ASK Whitedove

Psychic Insights From Angels to Zodiac

Volume 1

ASK Whitedove

Spiritual Advice from America's Top Psychic Michelle Whitedove.

Psychic Insights From Angels to Zodiac

Michelle Whitedove

WHITEDOVE PRESS

In some instances the names have been changed to protect individuals privacy.

Whitedove Press
2728 Davie Boulevard, #226
Fort Lauderdale, FL 33312

www.MichelleWhitedove.com

To order additional copies of this book 310-350-5370

Book Design by Gary Marshall

Front Cover Photo Maliena Slaymaker
Author Photo Christine Kilger
Back Cover Photo Shanté Powders

Printed on Acid Free/Recycled paper
Printed in the USA

Library of Congress Control Number: 2012949811

ISBN# 9780971490864

First Edition

10 9 8 7 6 5 4 3 2 1

Whitedove Press titles:

Spiritual Development Series

SHE TALKS WITH ANGELS,
a psychic medium's guide into the Spirit World

ANGELS ARE TALKING,
a psychic medium relays messages from the Heavens

Children's Series

MY INVISIBLE FRIENDS: ANGELS
(a children's book)

ANGELS OF THE OCEANS,
DOLPHINS, WHALES, AND MERMAIDS
(forthcoming children's book)

Ghost Series

GHOST STALKER,
a psychic medium visits America's most Haunted Sites

GHOST STALKER II,
a psychic medium visits Europe's most Haunted Castles

Your Souls' Purpose?
Growth and Transformation!
So fly, fly butterfly!
- Whitedove

Introduction

I have a blinking sign above my head "Get Counseling Here!" Even as a twenty year old business owner, strangers would come into my shop and pour their hearts out. By way of intuition, my psychic guidance would always make the person feel better. All the while, I never revealed the fact that I was psychic. To my clients, it just seemed like sage advice.

As the owner of a nail and hair salon, my customers were mostly women. One day as I held the unpolished hand of a new client I blurted out "Your husband is on the other side?" I questioned myself in that moment. Logically it didn't make sense because she was young. But then a vision of her husband's death played out before me just like a TV clip on the evening news. Clearly I saw her husband at the moment of his death and how he was murdered at sea. Fortunately, my new client was more than grateful for the message of love and hope from the other side.

Once I came out of the closet as a professional Psychic Medium, I've never looked back. In fact, through a series of synchronicities I was on the fast track to develop my gifts to an entire new level. A local cable TV station wanted to have a psychic show on air and so they contacted a new age bookshop where I gave classes. The owner highly recommended me for the job. After a brief interview with the producer, I was offered my own show to give spiritual counseling on Live TV. I was saying yes to the Universe and the divinely orchestrated path was opening.

We each have a mission and a purpose. When God places signs in front of us; we just have to say "Yes" and move forward. This was my first big career challenge and spiritual test. I was so nervous and could have easily said "No," because they were asking me to do so many things that I had never done before. And on LIVE TV, yikes!

Fear is not your friend. In fact, fear is the very opposite of love. When we are divinely guided we must be strong and walk through our fears. This was an exciting new endeavor, although at this point in my career all my clients had come to my office for readings and spiritual counseling. Now I was being asked to take calls in rapid succession as a psychic medium, and learn how to do live TV: talk into the camera without blinking a million times, pay attention to camera changes, cues for commercial breaks and read a teleprompter for my show opening and closing remarks. I said a prayer of gratitude and walked through the fear. In life, once you meet the challenge then you will find a great sense of accomplishment and satisfaction on the other side of fear.

As I walk this journey called life, I have repeated this cycle of following my intuition and taking on tasks that I thought were near impossible. "America's Psychic Challenge" and "Sixth Sense International" tested my abilities and my faith, these feats allowed me to continue to learn and spiritually grow by leaps and bounds. This is a life lesson for everyone; remember to be receptive, positive, open minded and walk through your fears. Earth is a school house and we come here to learn difficult lessons.

Sharing the wisdom teachings from Heaven is my mission and purpose. I was born this way, a psychic medium with a clear connection to the Heavens. I have spiritually counseled tens of thousands of people across the globe from different cultures, income brackets and religious backgrounds. In this book ASK Whitedove, I share their interesting questions that are posed to me with straightforward answers and soul-solutions.

Sending you Love, Light and Peace,

Michelle Whitedove
www.MichelleWhitedove.com

Dedication

I dedicate this book to the Great Spirit, my Angels & Guides, through them all things are possible. A special thanks to Shanté for making this book happen, Caylee Hermelyn for editing and to Jason for his unwavering support.

Contents

Contents

The goal isn't to sit on a pile of gold. The goal is to stand upon your good deeds. You can't take the gold with you, although your deeds will follow you into the afterlife.

- Whitedove

A

Dear Whitedove,
Last year my husband and I became pregnant. Unfortunately I was told that the baby would be born with some major birth defects. Jointly we decided to abort and try again for a healthy fetus. Since then, I've had feelings of guilt and grief that my child is gone; now I wonder if what we did is a sin. Did we create negative Karma for ourselves by choosing abortion?
- *Not Perfect in Daytona*

Dear Not Perfect,
Even the bible tells us that the baby does not breathe its first breath of life until it is born. Just as we have different death dates, we also have different arrival dates. Sometimes a soul will choose to wait rather than to be born into a body that is physically or mentally dysfunctional. This does not mean that you will not have this soul at a later date. It may occur through a different pregnancy or maybe that soul will even use another mother as a birthing vehicle only to be adopted by you. Through my readings, "Spirit" addresses abortion as a choice and does not carry negative karma with it unless used inappropriately, like using **abortion** as a repeated form of birth control. Do not think of a

miscarriage or an abortion as a death; instead, remember that it is simply a delay. That soul will be waiting in the heavens for a better opportunity to come into a physical life.

Dear Whitedove,
I have two children who are in elementary school; one is doing fine, the other is struggling, and I am afraid that she is going to fail. Her teachers told me that I should put her on medication for Attention Deficit Disorder (ADD). What can I do?
- Panicked in Tulsa

Dear Panicked,
First of all, teachers should never be diagnosing their students, let alone suggesting treatment with drugs. They are not doctors. I am very much against drugging our children; it is not the solution, just another problem. If you just research the side effects of the Psychotropic Drugs used for **ADD / ADHD**, this should be enough to deter you. As a Health Intuitive, I see that there are not only terrible side effects for long term use for the physical body, but also for the spirit. Your child is most likely an indigo child, a very highly evolved spiritual soul. These amazing children

need a lot more one on one attention to get through their education. When I have clients that come to me with their Indigo children, I always recommend that they consider placing their child into a Waldorf or a Montessori school. These school areas are designed to give children much needed one on one attention, the class room sizes are smaller, and the education is superior. For those parents who are able to stay at home with their kids, they may tackle home schooling. I know many parents who have opted to home school and I feel it is also a viable way to ensure your children get the best education possible. Psychotropic Drugs should be used with great caution.

Dear Whitedove,
There's a lot of hype about whether or not Aliens really exist. My family believes that the idea of life on other planets is just science fiction; but I've always thought they're real.
- *Lucky Stars in Key West.*

Dear Lucky,
It would be very presumptuous of us to look up to the Heavens at night to see the sky beaming with stars only to assume that Earth is the only planet with life. There

are most definitely other forms of intelligent life which I prefer to call "Star Beings" instead of **aliens**. Humans must open their hearts and minds to realize that just because we cannot see something doesn't mean that it does not exist. Science recently discovered planets in neighboring galaxies that they call "Super Earths" and look to be more than capable of sustaining different life forms. Hopefully the human race will learn to accept Star Beings as common knowledge, thus opening us up to new possibilities, perhaps even contact.

Dear Whitedove,
I want to know if I saw an eight foot tall Angel. Please tell me what they look like.
- Seeing Things in Australia

Dear Seeing,
Angels show themselves very rarely although there are a great many among us. Many legions have come to help create a sense of balance where there has been a great imbalance. I have seen a very large Angel like the one that you described. They are very tall and leave a glowing residue of pulsating light after they disappear. An angel sighting is a great blessing and you will feel humbled by

the awe of your encounter.

Dear Whitedove,
Can we have animals that act as our spirit guides? Whenever I pray and try to picture my guides I always see a great white horse. What does this mean?
- *Projecting Visions in Long Beach*

Dear Visions,
Animals do not act as direct Spirit Guides; they are what I call our totem helpers. We all have two **animal totems** that stay with us throughout our lives. We also have other animal totems that will be in our life for a period of time usually to help us with a particular issue, or lesson, and then leave when we have overcome it. When you have Horse as an animal totem, it symbolizes "Freedom, Power, Healing and Astral Travel." For a more elaborate explanation, there is a book by Ted Andrews called "Animal Speak" which gives you an index listing of all sorts of different animals and what they mean when you see them enter your life. Always pay attention to your animal totems, they will be a great strength to you when you need it the most.

Dear Whitedove,
Recently, I was told that I have St. Anthony around me. Why is that? And is he also an angel?
- Protected in Pittston

Dear Protected,
Saint Anthony is not an Angel, he is the Patron Saint for the poor, travelers, and he is in charge of recovering lost items. In life he lived such a pure and selfless existence, that less than one year after his death he was granted sainthood by the pope. Many times in order to determine saint hood, the church will exhume bodies looking for a sign or a miracle. When St. Anthony's body was exhumed it was said that his tongue was still perfect in color and shape, even moist at glance. When we need help here on Earth we usually will pray to God, our Angels and our Spirit Guides. Saints are other heavenly helpers that we can pray to for assistance. For you, call on St. Anthony to help you locate an important lost item and he will help you find it!

Dear Whitedove,
I own an antique store and after a recent shipment of merchandise, I've noticed that strange unexplainable things have begun to happen: lights flickering, books falling, and items missing and then reappearing. Is my store haunted?
- *Spooked in TN*

Dear Spooked,
Your problem is not a haunted location, but a haunted thing! Ghosts and entities not only haunt places; they can also become attached to their personal possessions. This can hold true for **antiques**. Chances are in your last shipment you received more than your normal every day merchandise. Since this spirit is obviously creating havoc for you, I would suggest going through your shipment and trying to locate the source of your haunt; it should feel different, it will have a heavier energy to it when touched. You can either return it, or dispose of it to someone who is aware of the situation. It would not be nice to sell that item to a customer who was clueless. Until you solve this issue, I suggest clearing and blessing your store to try and keep your mishaps down to a minimum. Burn white sage and smudge your store. Then place kosher salt in all four corners of each room. This will raise the vibration of your personal space.

Dear Whitedove,
My friend is an Atheist. What happens to people who have no faith or belief in God?
- White light in OR

Dear White light,
Just because you can't see an electric current, doesn't mean that it won't affect you, right? Science has proven that we are energy, and energy can never die. People don't have to believe in energy. Great Spirit never forces us to believe in anything; for Free-Will is our birthright. Our soul moves from one plane of existence to the next. When the soul enters the transition that we call death, we come into a state of knowing, like a veil has been lifted and we can see clearly and we know the truth. So don't worry, and don't preach, just be an example of God working through you. **Atheists** will find the truth on the other side of life.

Dear Whitedove,
You spoke at a local expo where they were doing aura photography. As an artist, I was intrigued by

the colors and their size. What is your explanation of an aura?
- An Artist in Miami

Dear Artist,
These specialty photos capture your bio magnetic field on film. I call the **aura**, "the Over-soul;" it's the part of the soul that can be seen. Did you know that in the spirit world we are known by our colors and rank? The colors of an Aura all have significant meaning. During the Renaissance Period angels were depicted with halos in paintings. But the viewer had misinterpreted what he was seeing. The crown chakra is the strongest and angels imitate the golden light of Heaven, therefore their aura is always a golden color. During our time, there is a group known as the indigo children, they are advanced souls who incarnated to help humanity evolve, and their Auras are a bluish-purple. Most people have two or three colors in their aura at all times, so I hope that you had your photo taken.

When you freely give your time, your money, and/or your prayers to someone in need ...
you also gift yourself.
- Whitedove

B

Dear Whitedove,
That old saying applies to me; if it weren't for bad luck, I'd have no luck at all. How can I become lucky in a positive way?
- *Lady Luck in PA*

Dear Lady Luck,
Many people believe that being lucky is random, but actually a force that's within each of us. Your belief system creates your life, and what you think about will manifest. You have bought into a self fulfilling prophecy of **bad luck**. But once you recognize this pattern, you can reprogram your beliefs and develop a positive outlook on your future. Retrain your brain to expect good. Clean up your negative mind chatter and replace those thoughts with loving, positive, motivational phrases. Be kind to yourself and know that you are worthy. Your luck is now changing, there is power in positive thinking. When you shift your thoughts from fear and lack to thoughts of love, miracles happen.

Dear Whitedove,
This is a weird question but I'm sure that you get them

all the time. This morning, I took my dogs outside as usual. As I stood there, a little bird (a Wren) started to fly around me. It was flying low, then high and swooping down to get my attention. It was really a very cool experience. I feel blessed because it went on for a long while untill it landed on the fence and was just watching me. It was like the little bird was trying to tell me something. Any insight?
- Feathered Friend in Miami

Dear Friend,
There's truth to the saying "a little birdie told me." Every animal has a message: Native Americans call it a medicine. Spiritually speaking **birds** represent flight to the higher realms. So it's good that you saw the fly-by as a good omen and message. When you are able to identify the type of bird, you can then hone in on the individual meaning. Here are some to remember: The Dove represents peace and prophecy, the Hummingbird represents joy and new relationships, the Crow is about magic, the Hawk is a warning to be more aware and your little Wren is a message to be resourceful and bold. So take note and continue your friendship with nature.

Dear Whitedove,
There is a famous hotel in my area that boasts of a nightly apparition of a woman descending a staircase. My question is this: Why would a ghost be compelled to spend time doing such repetitive actions?
- Scientific Mind in Miami

Dear Scientific,
Well, this type of paranormal activity is often mistaken for a ghost, although it's actually called a **"bleed-through."** This is when a scene plays itself out much like a holographic movie clip. It's literally a scar on the fabric of time. When a heartbreaking event takes place, the strong energy of the incident can leave an impression on time. It plays itself out night after night at a specific time until it fades away. The scene is always the same, there are no variations. These "bleed-throughs" happen all over the world. In ancient Rome, there is a corridor where the legions of soldiers are seen marching to their death. The action still plays out although the souls have long ago moved on.

Upon death, we come into a state of awareness and know that the body was only a temporary vehicle to house the soul during this short journey to Earth.

- Whitedove

C

Dear Whitedove,
I was at a ceremony the other day where they were burning sage to cleanse the space. I find it hard to believe that smoke is cleansing. Is it just a wives tale or is there truth in that smelly smoke?
- *Clean Freak in Boston*

Dear Clean Freak,
From ancient times sacred smoke has been used to lighten the energy and consecrate areas or even objects. Many religious ceremonies use incense made of resins and spices such as frankincense as a conduit to Heaven. The Native Americans smoked a peace pipe and their prayers were carried to the Great Spirit in the rising smoke of tobacco. Smudging with sacred smoke is used to clear negativity, clear energy fields, to raise the vibration and bless the space. You do this by lighting the Sage, Cedar, and/or Bear Root then extinguish the flame. Use the smoldering smoke by fanning it into the room in a clockwise manner, all while giving thanks to the sacred plants and to the Great Spirit. You can perform your very own sacred **ceremony**.

Dear Whitedove,
What does the color purple mean in spiritual terms? Is it true that we are known in the Heavens by our soul's colors?
- *Colorful in Corvallis*

Dear Colorful,
Purple is the highest spiritual **color**; if you see purple in a person's aura, then it means they are very spiritually evolved. Yes, in the Heavens we are known and ranked according to our colors. This also means that as our souls evolve, our colors will also change.

Dear Whitedove,
Since I was a small child I have loved stones. Is there a spiritual connection to Rocks, Minerals, and Crystals?
- *A Rock Hound*

Dear Rock Hound,
Yes, there is a reason that you've been attracted to the very essence of Mother Earth. Each stone has its own special attributes and they are alive with healing properties. Many Ancient civilizations knew the power of **crystals** and

harnessed it. There are many types of crystals that are used to power watches, radios, and computers. I'd suggest that you seek out a teacher or tutor that specializes in the energy of stones.

Dear Whitedove,
I recently read some stuff on the power of crystals and how they can help heal the body. Could this possibly be true? I'm very spiritual, but this seems far fetched even for me.
- Skeptical in Seattle

Dear Skeptical,
Crystals and most specifically Quartz, carry a very high vibration within its minerals which act as a conductor for actual healing to occur. Crystals are an extremely strong energy force on Earth and if used correctly, can heal, and in general, harmonize those that use them by helping the energy in our bodies to better flow through us. This use of **crystal healing** has been around for thousands of years. Although it is not a treatment, I would recommend it for any severe illness; it most definitely helps promote the healing process.

What is true enlightenment?
It is a state of being, a state of
knowingness by mastering
unconditional love and grace
while being in the physical body.
- Whitedove

D

Dear Whitedove,
My father died about ten years ago and our family really misses him. But I'm troubled that my sister always prays to him. How do you feel about praying to dead loved ones?
- Daddy's Girl in Missouri

Dear Daddy's Girl,
From the other side, our loved ones do check in on us from time to time for **death** is not the end. Deceased family members are limited in their abilities to actually assist us because they are still healing, learning and evolving in the spirit realm. I would ask you to pray for him, not to him.

God has given us an unseen support team of Angels and Guides of helpers. I always advise people to take their prayers and requests to the top. God is the all knowing Universal Consciousness that has the solutions to our Earthly problems.

Dear Whitedove,
In your book, you wrote about our soul contract

and our death date. I was wondering, can a tragedy really be an accidental death or is our destiny always written? I'm amazed that the accident rate is ever increasing. Does this play a part in our soul's contract?
- Statistically Challenged in Maine

Dear Statistics,
It's hard to fathom how much preparation goes into planning our journey to Earth. We create a road map of the intended trip and we make agreements to fulfill certain obligations along life's journey. We choose a birth date as a starting point and we also create several possible exit dates. In most cases, the timing for death has been selected based on the soul's evolution. God calls us home at the right time. So yes, there are several **death dates**. Also, there are rare events where a soul's "free will" has interfered with another's and they have been taken prematurely. This is one of the reasons that there is an increase of Near Death Experiences. It's essential that souls stay and complete their mission. Just think about how many people that you come in contact with during the course of a lifetime. All of your interactions affect the people that you touch and the domino effect continues. The smallest gesture can change the world. This is why each soul is so much more powerful than you realize.

Dear Whitedove,
I had a dream about a deceased relative, and when I woke up I swear I could smell her perfume. Is there a logical reason for that?
- *Nostalgic in Orlando*

Dear Nostalgic,
Many times our **deceased loved ones** will come through to visit us in the dream state. Just because we don't always consciously remember what they are saying to us, it is their way of letting us know they are still with us, watching over us. Those dreams are a blessing and a gift. Please know that your departed loved ones really are visiting you from the Heavens.

Dear Whitedove,
How did you interpret the end of the Mayan Calendar on December 21st 2012? What did this mean for us? Obviously it was not the end of the world.
- *Prayerful in Puerto Rico*

Dear Prayerful,

The Mayans were advanced in reading the stars and predicting the future based on astronomy and Divine messages. In ancient times, they recorded the future up to this specific time; then they saw that mankind's free-will would determine the future from the point of the Great Cosmic Awakening. Their calendar marked a time, **December 21, 2012** when the entire Universe comes into a state of change. It's not the end of the world, but a new beginning. Know that you incarnated during this time to ring-in this special era of human history! Currently we are at a critical tipping point. We are creating our future as we move forward, so each of us must be consciously responsible for the part that we play in this Great Awakening. Ask yourself: What do I want to create? Individually your thoughts create your future; the mass consciousness creates a larger reality. I encourage everyone to monitor your thoughts because they are the building blocks that help to construct your future. Delete the negative mind chatter; stay positive and pray about the good that you want to bring into the world. Then take action, with kindness and generosity of spirit, help your fellow man. Use your words to bless, educate, and heal. You are powerful beyond measure.

Dear Whitedove,
I've had several instances of déjà vu, the feeling that I am re-experiencing an event or conversation. How do you explain these types of happenings?
- *Familiar Stranger in CA*

Dear Familiar,
The concepts of Time and Space can be difficult to wrap your head around. "Spirit" has explained to me that our past, present, and future, are all one. Time is like an onion, with many layers of actual events and possible futures. As the mass consciousness changes, so does our future. It's important to recognize that humans are multi-dimensional beings who are in charge of creating their reality. Science is even considering the theory of parallel universes.

When you experience **déjà vu,** your mind is connecting with the event as a memory. In linear Earth time, the event must occur in sequence. On a higher level of awareness, your soul connects to this event with familiarity because you have already experienced it. Now you are just going through the physical motions.

There is also "Past Life" déjà vu that many people experience when traveling abroad. We are sometimes drawn to places where we experienced a past incarnation. Your past life memory triggers this type of déjà vu. For example: You go to Egypt for the first time, yet you are familiar with the many places that you visit without prior knowledge.

Dear Whitedove
Every single person that I speak to is somewhat depressed. Even I have experienced depression from time to time, although I don't have any major issues going on right now. Is there a spiritual reason for this?
- Depressed in Detroit

Dear Depressed
Remember we are all brothers and sisters; we are all truly connected! Collectively, on a soul level, we sense the troubles befalling humanity, hence the reason for your **depression**. The Native American people refer to this as "The Web;" no matter what part of the web is touched, it ripples down and we all feel it. Our minds and hearts are connected because we are all sparks of the Great Spirit! Use prayer and meditation to help sooth yourself. Stay away from the negative people and places and use your light to help others. In this way, you will help lighten the load and make our world a better place.

Dear Whitedove,
Our family dog just died and we miss her so much. Do good dogs go to heaven?
- *Dog-goned in FL*

Dear Dog Lover,
Our canine companions are Earth Angels that are highly evolved souls. They are here to teach mankind the value of unconditional love. **Dogs** are truly man's best friend and they represent the finest attributes of loyalty, faithfulness & service. That's why they lend themselves in service as: cadaver dogs, k-9 police dogs, search and rescue, bomb and drug sniffing, helping the blind and hearing impaired, and even seizure alert dogs. Dogs have proven to be of great service to man and these are their natural characteristics. They lead us by example. All animals have souls and yes, all dogs go to Heaven! In fact, our loved ones and often our pets are there to greet us on the other side when we return to our true home.

ASK Whitedove

Dear Whitedove,
I often see large pods of dolphins here on the Baja coast. Every time that I am outside they seem to come to greet me. I really love them, but how could they know that? What is this connection that I feel?
- *Beloved in Baja*

Dear Beloved,
Dolphins have a special affinity with humans; they are the Angels of the Oceans. Science has proven that these mammals have superior intelligence. Man has discovered that dolphins can be effective when used as therapy mammals for people with unique mental capacity such as: autism, Down syndrome, slow learners, and others that are labeled as intellectually challenged. There is so much that science has not discovered. Dolphins understand us, and even know our intent. These Angels have special healing gifts and psychic communication abilities since they are multi-dimensional beings. As Angels of the oceans, they have come here to Earth to assist humankind in bodies that are a type of disguise. These dolphins know that you love and appreciate them. You can call on them through your prayers and in your mediations. Right now, it's important that we pray for them! If the pollution and poisoning of the Oceans continues, their physical bodies will not be able to survive. I ask all people to pray for the

Oceans, the sea life, the mammals, the living reefs, and the whales too. Our sea life is a vital key to the wellbeing of humankind. It's too bad that science hasn't come to this important conclusion.

On stage – Sydney, Australia

Today come from LOVE
in everything that you
DO and SAY.
Give it a try.
- Whitedove

E

Dear Whitedove,
Gosh there have been so many Earthquakes recently. Are we more aware because the news media is instantaneous or is there something else going on?
- *Quaking in CA*

Dear Quaking,
The fear based media conglomerates are happy to send doom and gloom reports around the world. There is much more important Spiritual News to report. This is a very important time for light workers to be active in daily prayer, meditation, and be in service to humanity. We are in a time of great **Earth Changes.** Mother Earth is in a cleansing process and she's trying to shake off the negativity. The quakes, volcanoes, and storms will increase; this is nature's way of clearing, purging, and wiping away all that does not serve this living breathing planet. The good news: on the other side of nature's demolition, the Earth will come into a time of renewal and rebirth eventually.

Dear Whitedove,
I was told that the recent solar eclipse in Asia is

going to bring about a lot of hard times for people in their relationship area. Why do things keep getting more and more difficult?
- Frustrated in Franklin

Dear Frustrated,
The Solar **Eclipse**, in astrological terms, happens to hit our relationship aspect (varying according to how your chart is mapped out.) You may be confronted with many issues relating to your loved ones, partners, friends, etc. We have begun the Ascension, which means Mother Earth is cleansing herself. People are now clearing up as much karma and as many life lessons as possible during this time. The Solar Eclipse is just one of the many ways these changes are facilitated. Sometimes being in the flesh makes it difficult for us to proactively grow on a spiritual level; often we need a nudge in the right direction. Events like a Solar Eclipse are not punishment, but instead an opportunity to grow. Look at your personal relationships on all levels and decide what needs to be done to improve them. Instead of being so fearful of the coming changes that you miss your window, try taking a moment to be thankful for the chance to improve your life.

Dear Whitedove,
With the holidays coming up and all the news reports saying that our economy is only going to get worse, I'm afraid to spend money unless absolutely necessary. If my husband were to lose his job on Wall Street we would be in financial ruin. Spiritually speaking, what can I do to prepare?
- *Scarce in Manhattan*

Dear Manhattan,
First of all, be thankful for the things you do have in your life instead of worrying about the things you don't. Christmas is a time to be joyful for family and to show love to those in your life; not so much through the giving of expensive gifts but through the enjoyment of a quiet time together for celebration, laughter, and love. There is so much fear in the world right now, please don't help feed the fear. Clinging on to a bit of Christmas money will not save you from drastic financial difficulty or a failing **economy**. You have to trust that Spirit will take care of your needs and help you. When we hang onto money too tightly, we are saying that we do not trust spirit. I am not telling you to spend your money frivolously, but sometimes you have to give in order to receive; it's the natural flow of the Universe.

ASK Whitedove

Dear Whitedove,
I recently discovered my spiritual path but my boyfriend wants nothing to do with it and no matter what I try, I can't seem to convince him otherwise. How can I get him to be more spiritual?
- *Convinced in St. Pete*

Dear Convinced,
It's great that you found your spiritual path, however spirituality comes from within, you cannot force it on someone else. Either your boyfriend will discover his own spirituality or he won't, but either way you need to honor his freewill. If you try to force it on him, you will only push him further away. The best thing that you can do is stay on your path and incorporate spirituality in your everyday life to set a good example for him. Know that many times we outgrow our relationships as we move forward on our path. If you really want to help your boyfriend, then pray for him, and ask his unseen support team to help him find his way. Opportunities for growth will present themselves, but the rest is up to him. I always tell people there is no magic pill for instant **enlightenment**, we all have to do the work.

Dear Whitedove,
For my birthday I received a necklace that contained an evil eye pendant on it. It is very pretty but I've heard a lot of conflicting information on its true purpose. So I'm a bit nervous to wear it.
- Cautious in Cleveland

Dear Cautious,
The **evil eye** dates back to ancient times, when it was believed that certain people had the ability to curse you or cause you misfortune just by staring at you. Usually it is caused by jealousy and envy of the good fortune someone else is having. This belief was so profound on ancient cultures that the Egyptians began wearing ornate eye makeup as a way to ward off evil stares. In more modern times the concept of wearing eyeliner was converted into charms of protection, hence the "Evil Eye" charm. There is nothing wrong with wearing your evil eye necklace. It is a positive power object that will add protection to the wearer, because like many power symbols the evil eye is strongly believed and trusted in that our vibration and thoughts has made it so. Remember we have the gift of co-creation, if you believe it, then it is relative because you give it power.

Dear Whitedove,
I have a nephew that is 10 yrs old and for the last year, he has turned into a different person; he acts like he is possessed. We've tried counseling, a new school, and nothing has worked. I've had readings from different prominent psychics who all say that there is an entity attached to him. Should we look into an exorcism, and if so how would we do that?
- Desperate in Detroit

Dear Desperate,
Possessions are rare, but should be taken very seriously. **Exorcisms** should be used only when you are absolutely positive that there is an entity attached to the child. To my knowledge, Priests of the church no longer conduct exorcisms. You will need to seek a Spiritual Medium or a Shaman who has the ability and willingness to perform an exorcism. For the time being, make sure that your nephew's family is "clearing and blessing" their home daily to keep the vibration as high as possible. To ensure the safety of your nephew and the family, please do not attempt to exorcise an entity by yourself, it can be dangerous. If you are interested in more information feel free to contact my office; in the mean time you and your family will stay in my thoughts and prayers.

Special Event at Lily Dale

You are most open and receptive during the dreamtime. Your soul is free from physical and intellectual constraints.

- Whitedove

F

Dear Whitedove,
I've read that "any" act of Faith will bless us, is this true?
- *Faithful Follower in NYC*

Dear Follower,
The word **FAITH** says that you are very hopeful. It's positive but there is an element of reservation or doubt. I'd suggest that you move into a place of certainty and conviction. Your belief is strongest where there's a deep sense of knowing. Once you stop doubting, your blessings will multiply rapidly!

Dear Whitedove,
I am wondering what people are talking about when they refer to the Fairy Kingdom. I have to admit the idea is intriguing, but I've never seen a fairy flitter by me either. On the other hand, I don't see how it's much different to believe in fairies than angels. Please shed some light on this for me.
- *Cosmically Confused in CA*

Dear Cosmically Confused,
I can understand how people would misconstrue the idea of the **fairy kingdom** into some out of this world fantasy fest, but that is not what we mean when we refer to the Fairy Kingdom. The fairy kingdom consists of all spiritual creatures that are earthbound, this means, Elemental Spirits, (meaning spirits governed by the Elements of Earth such as water, air, fire) the animals, plants, and of course the ever elusive fairies (also known as the angels of the Earth.) Not everyone will see Tinkerbelle flying by with a sparkly wand, but their energy exists here just the same. They are in charge of protecting and aiding Mother Earth and all her inhabitants. Children are much more apt to see these spirits as their minds have not been programmed to disbelieve. I cannot stress enough to people that just because something is not in your view, doesn't mean it does not exist.

Dear Whitedove,
Everywhere I turn I see the world in crisis. The media is always talking about natural disasters, food shortages, and unclear water. I'm scared all the time; are we doomed? What can I do to not be so fearful?
- Frightened in Fresno

Dear Frightened,

Fear does nothing but create the very thing you are scared of. There are many parts of the world right now that are plagued with natural disasters and we need to come together as light workers and find ways to fix what we have broken. We have allowed the Earth to be polluted and the natural disasters we are seeing are in large, a result of this. Imagine if each person had the same fear as you, took that energy and instead of worrying, began to pray and work toward solutions; it would be amazing how quickly things would turn around. Trust in your connection to Spirit to help guide you to making good decisions that will keep you out of harms way as well as protecting the planet. Pray for Mother Earth and all her children, recycle, make your home energy efficient, car pool, and don't litter. Be prepared for the worst but always pray for the best. Hording food, and living in fear will only help bring that fear to life. Instead be smart about your house hold supplies; keep a small supply of canned foods and bottled water, but do it openly and light heartedly so that the universe creates that abundance for you. See yourself being safe and happy. Like the old saying goes, "you bring about what you think about."

Dear Whitedove,
I recently went to a local psychic for a reading; I was disturbed by the fact that it seemed too general, as nothing was specific. Could you tell me what to watch for to avoid future frauds?
- *Sincerely Duped in Denver*

Dear Duped,
There are many wonderful psychics, but remember, there are frauds in every profession. Often a **fraudulent psychic** will appear to be accurate, when in fact they are performing what is referred to as a "Cold Reading." This is when they watch your body movement, your facial emotion and allow you to guide them to the correct answer. To avoid falling victim to a psychic fraud, first do your homework; make sure the psychic has a good reputation. Other warning signs are: If they ask you a lot of questions when you sit down with them, or if the person asks for large sums of money to clear up a problem. Hope this helps and good luck to you.

Dear Whitedove,
It seems the further along the spiritual path I get, the more long standing friends leave my life. It's confusing to me, although I understand my path

is not necessarily their path. Sometimes it can be lonely, but I am no longer happy with their way of life; I would not want to go back to it. Does this happen to everyone and how do I handle it?
- *Lonely in Boca*

Dear Lonely,
As you move along your spiritual path, you'll learn and grow. This means outgrowing belief systems that no longer serve you and creating new ones. You my friend, are going through a spiritual evolution. Likewise the World is in a quickening phase; on a subconscious level, humankind is working on their karmic lessons. You will find that people are coming in and out of your life like a revolving door. It's not just you. My advice is to honor those old **friends**, bless them and move on. What about the new people that you are attracting? Look into their eyes and be present during your interactions. Ask yourself: "What am I to learn? What lessons am I teaching?" Without judgment you can be at peace with your evolving relationships.

When we are feeling lonely, this is a call to action; to remove the focus from "Self," just jump in and help another. Get involved, from random acts of kindness to devoting yourself to a cause. This involvement will also become a catalyst for other doors to open. This is a universal truth for all.

Prayers make a huge impact on outcomes. Don't let a low opinion of yourself get in the way. Your prayers DO make a difference.

- Whitedove

G

Dear Whitedove
I was at a spiritual retreat and someone said that we all have a gate keeper. I was wondering if you've heard the term "Gate Keeper" and if so, could you explain in more detail.
- *Perplexed in Carlisle*

Dear Perplexed,
Every person on Earth has an "Unseen Support Team" on the other side. Your **Gate Keeper** is part of your team of Angels and Spirit Guides who walk through this life to help you and guide you on the right path. Your Gate Keeper's specific job is to protect your personal space in the spiritual realms. For example, if a deceased loved one wished to come to you through the dream state or even on a rare occasion physically manifest, they would need permission from your Gate Keeper. This specific helper knows your safety zone. They work very diligently to make sure your boundaries are not violated, and that nothing from the other side whether positive or negative can have access to you unless it is what you need or desire. Gate Keepers provide many obstacles for remote viewers as well; someone who tries to physically spy on another person will often feel the wrath of their Gate Keeper. They also keep evil entities

at bay; your Gate Keeper is on the constant look out, like your own spiritual body guard. As such, you should always recognize and give thanks to your Gate Keeper for the protection they provide you every single day of your life.

Dear Whitedove,
My husband is fascinated with several of the paranormal programs that focus on "Ghosts." Yet I'm not convinced that ghosts exist; there's such a lack of scientific evidence. Do you think that our loved ones are ghosts that peer in on us from time to time?
- Need more evidence, Georgia

Dear Needing,
Science tells us that we are made up of energy and you cannot destroy energy, this is a fact. Religion tells us that life continues after death. If you truly believe that life goes on, why is it so hard to believe in **Ghosts**? Let me explain the phenomena; at the time of death, God still honors our free will. Most souls drop their physical body and move into the Heavens, our true home. As we cross over, we become aware of the spirit world, and just follow the light. All souls are processed much in the same way as they enter Heaven. Our loved ones are

souls that are allowed to check on us from time to time and even visit us in the dream time. They would not be considered ghosts.

Then there are some souls that do not move into the light. They're called wayward spirits or ghosts. They actually turn away from the doors of heaven. I divide ghosts into two categories. The first are the ones who choose to stay. I've seen many reasons that a soul may want to stay here: out of great love for someone, out of fear for what awaits them, hatred, vengeance, love of a place or home, a need for justice, or another other strong human emotion that keeps them attached to the physical realm.

Then there are souls that stay earthbound for a period out of confusion. This happens many times after a traumatic death or suicide. When a soul is ejected from the body, it can be in a state of confusion or disbelief. Not realizing that the physical self is no longer a container for the soul, they wander about trying to live life as normal, although they realize that something's amiss. Know this: eventually all Earth-bound souls return to the heavens, some just take longer than others.

Dear Whitedove,
I saw you on TV and you spoke about your psychic abilities, God, and Angels. I feel that you have to be into religion to buy these invisible helpers. I'm agnostic and haven't ever felt comfortable with religion. Help me to understand.
- *Almost Atheist, UK*

Dear Almost,
There are many forms of life here on Earth and throughout the Universes. Angels are beings that are pre-religion, they have always existed. The one thing that all life forms have in common is that their core essence is pure energy.

As humans, we try to intellectualize everything. Does **God** look like us? Is he an all-knowing wise man with a beard? Are Angels male or female winged humanoids? We personify them to be like us, but actually they are energies. The Universal Consciousness is an energy force, the source of all things. Humans tend to compartmentalize and need to use labels: God, Allah, Great Spirit, Angel, whatever name that gives you comfort. When people see them, the human mind tries to establish their likeness from memory, just as we search a computer for a matching file. In actuality they are unique energy forms of light and superior intelligence.

At eighteen, I had a Near Death Experience at the scene of a fatal car crash. I had a personal encounter with Angels, and The Great Spirit. My energy/soul left my broken body and ascended. I found myself in the presence of the Universal Consciousness, which was so bright I couldn't look directly at it with my spirit eyes. In a telepathic manner, information is relayed.

This was a profound experience that I share with others so they may have faith that there is a greater force at work in the Universe. Please know that these energies do exist for you too. Anyone can call on them for assistance, with or without religious affiliations. That's the beauty, it's equal opportunity with the God force.

Dear Whitedove,
While so many people in the world seem to have had a horrible year, I actually feel that I have been very blessed. But I'm almost worried about my good fortune; I was thinking that I should volunteer or something to balance out my karma. What do you think?
- Humble in Houston

Dear Humble
I do not know why people think that if life's journey treats them well, that there will be some sort of punishment in store. Most people go through many trials and tribulations throughout their lives while others experience only a bit of negativity. It all depends on what you wrote into your life contract, what sort of reality that you are manifesting for yourself, and what karma you are working out. To answer your question, please go and volunteer this season when prompted to do so. My family and I always like to do some sort of charity a few times a year as it makes our hearts happy. Do it only because you truly want to help, not because you think you need to balance your karma. We are all brothers and sisters here learning together. What we do to each other we do to ourselves. There are no special rewards for living in poverty or wealth; it is what you do in any given situation that really matters. We come here to Earth to learn to give love freely, and many of us need to learn how to receive love. Give of your time, money, and talents with a joyful heart and be grateful for your **good fortune**!

Dear Whitedove,
My elderly aunt says that I have a Gremlin living in my house. This was her explanation for a bunch of

unrelated electrical issues in my home. I'm starting to wonder because at times my appliances work, then they will go on the blink.
- Mischief maker, Boston

Dear Mischief,
There are many realms that co-exist on planet Earth, some are visible, others are not. The Angel kingdom and the fairy realm are relatively unseen but they are among us. Your aunt is a wise woman; please listen to her so that this knowledge is not lost. **Gremlin** is a term for a playful little soul of the fairy kingdom, but don't worry, everything will be fine. These fun loving beings are meant to bring joy into your life, so just learn to laugh at the little inconveniences.

God is not a bearded man playing a harp while sitting atop of a cloud. God is an all-knowing, all powerful Divine Consciousness of Unconditional love. Earthly language fails to express the immense awesomeness!

- Whitedove

H

Dear Whitedove,
As an art student and Spiritualist can you offer insights into the golden Halo that is often portrayed above an Angel? Halo's are in so many paintings but I've never heard a spiritual explanation.
- Angel in waiting, AL

Dear Waiting,
Throughout the centuries religious icons from every sect have been adorned with a **Halo** in paintings. In Eastern art sometimes the whole body is encircled in a light that's called a Mandorla. Haloed figures such as Saints and Angels represented the divine were pictured with their aura glowing above their crown chakra. Angel's auras are truly golden yellow. All art is channeled and so artists are often Seers and they painted the aura's densest part encircling the head. In paintings, the halo is a symbol that always represents an enlightened one.

Dear Whitedove,
As a historical writer I research and write about people of the past. In your opinion, when I cross to

the other side, will I meet these people of History? Do people who have passed on care if they are remembered or not?
- Florida Writer

Dear Writer,
Speaking from my own encounter when I had a Near Death Experience; when we cross over we are greeted by our loved ones and members of our soul family initially. Of course Guardian Angels are present too. As we move forward in our Heavenly experience, we will see the many souls that were important to us during our Earthy journey, and even souls who we thought were merely a chance encounter. For you, a couple of the **historical figures** that you write of are from your soul family. And yes you will meet them again. Do souls care if they are remembered? In Heaven we drop our ego, but we are acknowledged for our deeds, selfless works for humankind, our thoughts and our words. It's much like a personal assessment of spiritual growth. Yes, souls are happy to be remembered for their positive impact accomplished during life on Earth.

Dear Whitedove,
Humans have such a great capacity for goodness. If we are all born from the Heavens, why do humans have the ability to commit evil acts?
- *Very Saddened in WV*

Dear Saddened,
Great Spirit is unconditional love and all things surrounding spirit are also of pure love. When we incarnate to Earth, we travel further away from the love of Great Spirit to a much lower plane of existence. The opposite of Love is Fear, and through fear comes hate, apathy, and violence. Evil plays a part in **human nature** because Earth is a realm of duality where each soul can create their personal Heaven or Hell. Remember, Spirit gave us the gift of Free-Will so that each soul would reconnect with the Divine Intelligence of its own choosing. We come to Earth to learn different lessons, but we do share one commonality, and that is to bring us closer to "Spirit". Live your life by the Universal Law of Unconditional Love, and remember that the light is always stronger than the dark. Don't believe me? Go into a room, turn the lights out and then light a single candle; you will see how a tiny bit of light can penetrate even the darkest room. So let your light shine!

Our true home is Heaven.
The journey to Earth is merely
a learning expedition.
- Whitedove

I

Dear Whitedove,
My daughter has always had an imaginary friend named Tina. The other day I asked about Tina and was told that she doesn't visit often. Has my daughter outgrown need for this type of companionship?
- Wondering about Tina, Tampa

Dear Wondering,
As we enter this world, we are gifted with guardian angels and spirit guides to accompany us. The laughter and smiles of babies attest to seeing them. Many toddlers maintain this relationship and openly communicate with these Heavenly helpers. Tina is one of your daughter's Guardian Angels. These angels manifest in forms that we best relate to; they are constant companions whose mission is to guide and guard their charges. As angels of light, their influence is always positive.

As children grow, they become domesticated and learn to accept society's teachings. "My you have a vivid **imagination**" and statements like these direct children towards a different belief system. By the age of eight, a large percentage of kids forget their angel friends. It's very important for mentors to encourage their children's spiritual development. Today there is a large population of Indigo Children that strive to keep their Heavenly connection. Everyone young and old has angel helpers; mostly they are an unseen support team, be assured that they are there for you.

Dear Whitedove,
My one year old daughter is constantly staring around the room pointing and laughing, but never at us. Is she seeing something we don't?
- Funny Kids in Seattle

Dear Funny,
Your daughter clearly sees her Angels and Spirit Guides. **Infants** are able to see through the veil that separates our world from the Spirit World. They are pure and innocent and have a strong connection to the Heavens. Imagine if you could physically see and speak with your guides and angels. It would make your spiritual journey so much easier and this would assist you in making much better choices.

Parents underestimate their children and often tell them that these sightings are their imagination, and in extreme cases, some will seek out mental health solutions because they're afraid that the child is hallucinating and hearing voices. Then drugs are introduced. It's very sad that out of ignorance, we can destroy this beautiful and natural connection that children have to the Heavens. The best gift that you could give your daughter is to encourage her to communicate with Guides and Angels so that she remains connected throughout her life.

Dear Whitedove,
In my job I am required to be creative and think outside of the box. Today I really feel inspired. Yet other days, I'm not dialed-in and connected. Where does inspiration come from?
- Active in Austin

Dear Active,
Inspiration is the driving force from God and his legions. It's a spark lit from within to drive you to be a better person, to be kinder to your family and friends, to participate in helping humanity and to create positive change. Inspiration is motivation to spread Great Spirit's unconditional love with others through deeds, written word, and art too. Even in your most difficult times you'll

feel the gentle push of inspiration and motivation from The Great Spirit and the Angel Kingdom leading you to hope and to the light.

Dear Whitedove,
I've always felt that I have a strong sense of intuitive guidance, although I sometimes doubt the information. How can I tell if the voice is my intuition or just my intellect?
~Doubting Thomas, Calgary

Dear Thomas,
Intuition is like a muscle that needs to be exercised. The more that you use it, the stronger that it becomes. We are all born with an inner guidance system. It's a small voice inside, or a knowing; it's always the first thing that pops into your mind. You don't have to think about it; the answer is just there. Some men call it a gut feeling. Whereas the intellect is the voice of reasoning, it weighs the information and then makes a decision based on your body of wisdom.

It would encourage you to practice listening to your **intuition**. Be in the NOW; be mindful of the intuitive information that you are receiving. Did you arrive at a decision, or was the answer given? Meditation is a tool that will help you to empty your thoughts and mind chatter to open yourself to hear solutions more clearly. God talks with all of us. We just have to listen.

Teaching – Key West, Florida

Even in your darkest hour,
you are never alone.
- Whitedove

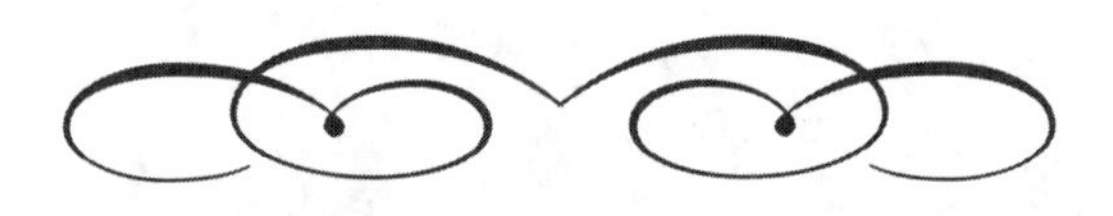

J

Dear Whitedove,
Can you please tell me if there is such thing as "Hands on Healing?" Is there a specific type that you would recommend, and what are your feelings on this subject?
- *Looking for Remedies in Maine*

Dear Looking,
There are many people on Earth that have an innate gift to use their own energy and essence to promote healing through touch; I refer to these souls as natural healers. Some of these methods are subtle and others are very profound. For example, Reiki is the simplest form of this "energy healing". The Reiki Master channels his or her energy into the receiver thus rejuvenating and alleviating symptoms of illness and stress. Then there are Massage Therapists who use their hands to pull out toxins in our bodies and relieve aches and pains, as well as realigning our energy. The rarest healers are known as the Master Healers such as **Jesus**, the Dalai Lama, and others. They have such a clear connection to "Spirit" that they can facilitate miracle healings just by being in their presence; they are pulling the pure love vibration of the "God Head" directly through them.

Just remember, as you are looking, please do your research in order to ensure that you're receiving the best treatment possible from someone who has a pure intent and who is qualified.

Dear Whitedove,
I had just been given several old pieces of jewelry from my father. My son took a well worn pair of cufflinks in his hand, when he looked up at me and said "these belong to Johnny, a man with a long white beard." I was stunned not knowing what to say. I called Dad to ask about the old cufflinks. He told me that they belonged to his Grandfather John, who was nicknamed Johnny when he was young. I'm still in shock, how did my boy receive information about his long dead relative?
- *Rocked Relative in MN*

Dear Relative,
Objects hold the vibrations of their past. A person can intuitively pick up on the impressions that emanate from an object. **Jewelry** can be a great conductor because it has sentimental attachments that are easily picked up on. This is called Psychometry; your small son is very intuitive

and with a little focus, he can develop his gifts fully. You should be open to hear his intuitions and encourage his natural psychic abilities.

Dear Whitedove,
My husband and I have been desperately trying to sell our home. I feel like we're never going to sell it for what it's worth, I'm ready to throw in the towel. Any advice on what we can do?
- Heartbroken in Madison

Dear Heartbroken,
This economic depression is hitting the real estate market hard and it may seem impossible to find a buyer for your home. As I tell my clients, you can not give into fear because you bring about what you think about. I'd suggest buying a small statue of **Saint Joseph**. Then bury him in your front yard with his head facing down and at a slight angle. Thank Great Spirit for the perfect buyer at the perfect price, and the perfect time. Do not ask for your home to sell, instead see it as already sold and give thanks. We need to learn to claim what we want, see it already being done and think positively. I realize that this can be difficult when we are surrounded by so much negativity but positive thinking

and level headedness will get you through difficult times much more successfully than a negative mindset. Work toward your goals, for your mind is the builder.

Dear Whitedove,
I've seen several curious notices in the newspaper "Thank you Saint Jude". Why the newspaper? And why the need to go public in such a formal way? I'd love to know.
- *Reading Papers in Chicago*

Dear Reader,
When praying to a Saint, you are asking the Saint to intercede, to petition God on your behalf. **Saint Jude** was one the twelve Apostles also called Thaddeus who's known as the "Saint of the Impossible!" He's the Saint to call upon when praying for the impossible, the helpless, or a hopeless cause. One thing that is certain: through God, all things are possible. When the prayer for the impossible is answered and a miracle is delivered, it's of popular belief that it's important to formally thank him. When you see postings in your local newspaper or on the internet this is a way to validate a person's sincere gratitude to Saint Jude in a public way. For those who

read the note of thanks it increases our faith knowing that miracles are achievable.

Sacred Sites Tour – England

The dreamtime is an automatic
doorway for our Angels,
Spirit Guides and loved ones
to visit with us.
Who are you dreaming of?
- Whitedove

K

Dear Whitedove,
The term KARMA is used often, but I am confused. Is there only bad karma? Or is there good karma too?
- *Cosmic Questioner, Miami*

Dear Cosmic,
"**Karma**" is relatively a new word for western civilization. You may understand the biblical term "reaping what you sow" or the new age phrase "the law of attraction." Science understands it as "the law of Cause and Effect." Simply put: For every action there is a reaction or similarly, for every cause there is an effect. This is a Universal truth in positive and negative aspects.

I consider "Good Karma" much like heavenly brownie points. Good deeds that flow in an unconditional manner will always be felt and recognized. You may not see the immediate effects, although during your life review you will have the opportunity and pleasure to see all the lives that you've touched. We are like pebbles that are cast into a pond...the ripples radiate out and touch everything! One small kind gesture can change a person's life, and thus change the world. Even a smile can generate change.

Negative Karma is something that we will need to revisit for our soul's growth. Please understand, there is no need for punishment in the heavens as we will choose to experience negativity so that we understand it, overcome it, and evolve spiritually.

Right now there is a great need to dwell in the positive, everyday strive to be of service. Look for opportunities to help another and lets all work to create more JOY in this world! Your actions make a huge difference.

Dear Whitedove,
I've had so many horrible things happen in my life even though I try to be a good person. My husband's sister is very selfish and uncaring yet she seems to have a completely charmed life. Why isn't the law of Karma applying here?
- Jilted in Jersey

Dear Jilted,
Karma is like a never ending debit card, pay now or pay later as no one is exempt, and don't forget that your good **karma** is repaid too.

In regards to your sister-in-law and her instant karma or lack there of, you have to understand that there's a bigger picture at work. Many karmic debts we pay back in our lifetime stem from what we created in previous lives. In other words, if you do something negative to a person in this life, you will most likely pay that karma back in a future life. Karma does not equate to being good or bad, it is simply a reaction to our actions. Another thing to remember is that we come to Earth to learn many lessons some of which are painful and unpleasant, but this does not automatically mean we deserve it or that we were paying back karma. For example, if you write in your life contract that you wish to learn the spiritual lesson of forgiveness, then you must have things happen in your life that would necessitate the act of forgiving. This is why it is so important to put our faith in Great Spirit and to always remember that we chose this life for our own soul's growth.

We must strive to stay away from judgment, only God knows the path of the soul's journey. My advice is to focus on your own spiritual growth, and let your family members work on theirs. Karma is an eternal equalizer.

Dear Whitedove,
What is the attraction and repulsion that pulls us strongly to some people and away from others? Does Karma play a part in our emotionally charged reaction to a so-called stranger?
- *Rekindled in Memphis*

Dear Rekindled,
Almost always the sort of attraction or repulsion between two people will stem from past life memories. When you meet a person that you instantly love and trust, chances are that they're from your soul clan, maybe a kindred spirit or even a soul mate (as we have more then one)! On the flip side when you meet someone that you instantly distrust or even dislike with absolutely no rational reason, usually this is a karmic bond from a past life. Perhaps that person had done you a disservice in a previous incarnation and your subconscious recognizes that soul's energy. And the imprint is still with you. This is often what makes it so difficult for soul's to repay karma owed. Remember that ALL Karma positive or negative must be repaid and reciprocated before the souls involved can move on from each other. In other words, if you do something wrong to a person in this life that you can not repay, then you will continue to meet them and work it out in future lives until you're able to

pay the debt. These are called **Karmic relationships**.

Lecturing in Pennsylvania

Intuition is the voice of God.
It is your inner guidance system.
- Whitedove

L

Dear Whitedove,
Here in the UK there is talk of special paths called Ley Lines. It is said that if you follow these pathways they will bring you prosperity and luck. I love taking long walks but is there any truth to this tale?
- *Doubtful Brit*

Dear Brit,
I have been to your Isle and have experienced many ancient Holy sites that are linked by these **ley lines**. To me they feel like power grids, a natural source of Earth Energy. I felt them strongly in Ancient Wilshire in the Southern portion of England where many crop circles appear. I felt the energy ley lines that run from Glastonbury, to Stonehenge to the Stone Circle of Avebury. They are straight lines of natural energy that connect sacred sites world wide. You must understand that these ancient sites were purposely built upon the ley lines. The lands were blessed with energy by God's hand, the blessings would extend to prosperity of body, mind, and Spirit.

Dear Whitedove,
Recently my mate died unexpectedly, and I feel such a heaviness and so very alone in this world. Have you ever been given proof that there is life after death?
- Longing to know in MA

Dear Longing,
The grief that you're feeling is a natural part of the healing process. We mourn, grieve and feel abandoned but grief is only for the living. Our loved ones are still with us, just in their lighter body. Did you know that the soul can travel at the speed of thought? Just concentrate your thoughts on that person and your loved one will come to you. They can hear you. However it's easiest for them to show themselves and interact in your dreams. These are actual visitations. For me, I have proof everyday; I see souls and they often ask me to relay a specific message. You will have your own experience through the dream time and it's a blessing when you feel reconnected, in this way you will know that there is **Life After Death**.

Dear Whitedove,
Some people believe that our life is mapped out

before we come to Earth and that is our fate. Others believe that we can change our life's path at any time. I would like to know is there a difference between fate and destiny or is our Life Mission pre-planned?
- Neptune's Girl, CO

Dear Neptune's Girl,
There is a great deal of planning that goes into a **life's mission**. As we prepare for our Earthly journey we make an agreement with God. We select lessons to learn and also lessons that we agree to teach others. We map out our journey and there are very few events etched in stone, but if there is something that we MUST experience; it's pre-ordained or called fate. Then there are other events that will only happen if everything is lined up with divine timing as destiny or a synchronicity. One of God's greatest gifts to humankind is the gift of free will. This affords us the opportunity to co-create our life on Earth. We can get caught up in drama and create a hellish life OR we can dream big and create personal heaven on Earth. Know this: your spirit has the ability to overcome any hurtle: poverty, abuse, illness or financial loss. Every great master has taught this truth. I would like to encourage everyone to monitor your thoughts because they are your building blocks. Visualize the future as you want it. Then take action. Heaven is within your reach!

Babies often see their Guardian Angels, you'll see them smiling and giggling at something unseen.

- Whitedove

M

Dear Whitedove,
There are several modern day magicians that perform amazing feats. I'd like to know is any of it real Magic?
- *Kreskin in AK*

Dear Kreskin,
From the beginning of time, mankind has the ability to create their desires with the force of their will. We are truly magical creatures; hence the very reason that the Angel Kingdom fell in love with man. There was a time in history that **magic** abounded. People could create and manifest with little effort because they KNEW that they could. Then we came into an era of logic, intellect, and higher learning. When this happened, our intelligence ruled and true magic was deemed impossible, so then trickery or sleight of hand became the new magic. Magic is real however, only a few have remembered how to harness their will to create change and manifest great feats. I Believe!

Dear Whitedove,
I've read about the Mayan calendar that ended

on Dec 21, 2012. Some say that it's the end of the world; others believe that this time represents a new beginning. What information have you received?
- An Avid Reader, FL

Dear Reader,
Much has been foretold in ancient prophecies. I have found that proper interpretation is the key to the true meanings. Through the ages, scribes and sages have translated sacred texts, but much is lost in translation. It's difficult enough to illuminate the meaning of ancient words in the correct context, because the Mayan wrote in glyphs, their words were in picture form.

The Mayan's were master astronomers who were devoted to astrology and many of their spiritual leaders were enlightened ones. They were able to predict their own future and could even see into our modern time. The **Mayan calendar** stopped on December 21, 2012 because their astronomers were aware of a major astrological occurrence, the signs pointed to a New Age, but the outcome was unclear. Their calendar ended at this time, the next evolution stage for mankind.

I predicted that this was not the end of the world, but the birth of a new paradigm. The shift in consciousness is already underway, and during the birthing process there are the pains of labor. We are in the midst of upheaval. The Mother Earth is molting and a portion of humanity is awakening, while others are resisting change.

God has bestowed two great gifts to humanity; the gift of co-creation and the gift of free will. Now is the time to use your gifts of manifestation. When you take away your fears, you possess the ability to create Heaven on Earth. This new age of enlightenment allows you to create your reality rather quickly, so monitor your thought patterns and dwell in the positive. Humanity needs to come away from the old programming and belief systems of fear and lack. I would suggest prayer, meditation and focusing on love. In this way your heart, mind, and soul is set free from the negativity that no longer serves you. I have been given much information about our future which I have written predictions in my two Angel books and my blogs so feel free to read them too.

Dear Whitedove,
In one week I had my computer break, lost an important contract for work, and my girlfriend and I have been fighting for days. A friend said it was

probably because of Mercury in Retrograde. If so, how does that work?
- ***Crazy Planet, Oakland CA***

Dear Planet,
Four times a year "**Mercury in Retrograde**" occurs. During this time the planet Mercury appears to be traveling backward through our solar system. Although retrograde is just an illusion, the effects still remain. All planets in our solar system go retrograde, but because Mercury is a very influential planet, astrologically speaking, it has a noticeable impact on humanity. Depending upon which sign Mercury is passing through at the time of retrograde you will notice conflicts arise in certain areas of your life. For example, if Mercury goes retrograde while in Libra you will notice difficulty in your relationship area as Libra rules that aspect. For the most part Mercury in retrograde will create chaos in your communications, potential turmoil in your relationships, and is even known to short circuit carious electronic equipment such like computers. While Mercury is in retrograde avoid signing contracts, dealing with relationship issues or even receiving surgery (unless it's absolutely necessary). Once you recognize the patterns, then you can plan accordingly. This is a time for us to lay low and to be watchful so that critical communication issues don't arise.

Dear Whitedove,
In my travels I have noticed some symbols that are repeated in different cultures. My friend was showing me pictures of sacred geometry but I think that I'm missing the point. Can you tell me the significance of Sacred Geometry?
- *Wandering Aussie*

Dear Aussie,
Sacred geometry is the Universal language of mathematical signs and symbols that create a higher vibration, frequency and harmony. The pyramid is the perfect example. One geometric symbol given by Archangel Metatron is particularly powerful; the Metatron Cube. **Metatron** is the archangel who sits at the throne and scribes for God. The 3-D Metatron Cube is sacred geometry that is the blueprint for all of creation, all life throughout the Universe. This is the symbol of creation that manifests: it acts as a shield to protect; it promotes abundance and good health. This cube is like a cell that advances growth on every level spiritually, physically, emotionally and mentally. You can utilize the Metatron cube as your personal shield of protection through visualization and prayer. Metatron says, "Very few will use this, but for those who do will reap the rewards." I can personally assure you that you'll see a vast and positive difference in your life.

The life review process is the most difficult part of our transition back home to Heaven. We experience all of the pain that we inflicted on others and we feel all of the joy that we gave. My advice, create Joy!

- Whitedove

N

Dear Whitedove,
Several people at my local New Age store use the greeting "Namaste". At the thought of sounding silly I was afraid to ask the meaning. Please shed some light on this welcome.
- *Spiritually Speaking in Norway*

Dear Spiritually Speaking,
You see, our words hold a vibration and a wise soul will use their words to heal, bless, and educate. **Namaste** is pronounced Nah-mah-stay: is a Sanskrit greeting of honor, respect, and prayerful reverence. This wonderful greeting conveys spiritual respect and offers a blessing to the recipient. One beautiful soul that I know greets everyone with "Hello Angel". She believes that this helps her friends and clients elevate their standards a little higher during their interaction. Don't you think that the world would be a better place if everyone would adopt a state of reverence in their greetings?

Dear Whitedove,
I have had a persistent health issue that's

bothersome but it's nothing major. My sister has been insisting that I make an appointment with a Naturopath. Do you think that this is wise council or will I just be wasting my time and money? I'm not interested in quackery.
- Looks like a duck in Denver

Dear Duck,
Never substitute quackery for professional medical advice, diagnosis or treatment. A Doctor of Naturopathic Medicine is accredited in the field of holistic medicine; I highly suggest that you find a Naturopath that you are comfortable with and one that has excellent credentials. There's an old saying "The physician treats, but it is Nature that heals."

Personally, I visit a Doctor that is a Pharmacist and a **Naturopath** because with her medical education I 'm always confident that she's knowledgeable in all aspects of Western medicine but she prefers the holistic methods of healing. In this way, I know I'm getting the best guidance. You need the same: a doctor with western medicine sensibility mixed with holistic solutions. It's time to get back to the basics with our health regiments. Intuitively we know that something's wrong when the drug company advertisements include a long list of side effects that are worse than the disease. Yes, I highly advise everyone to seek out a reputable Naturopath to give healthful guidance and remedies.

Dear Whitedove,
A close family member was hospitalized for a heart attack, thankfully he pulled through. He tells us that he had a heavenly experience during the ambulance ride: he saw angels and everything. Can someone actually experience Heaven while on Earth?
- *A Believer in Bellingham*

Dear Believer,
It's important to remember that you're a soul having a temporary experience on Earth. Yes, there are many documented cases of people having a **Near Death Experience**. When the physical body is in a state of severe trauma, the soul will eject. Some people who are resuscitated actually recall their journey of entering heaven; then ultimately their soul is restored to their body. The memory of this event is usually so profound it changes the person forever. Can you imagine being in the presence of Angels?

At eighteen, I had a NDE during a fatal car crash which I write about extensively in "She Talks with Angels". From first hand experience I can attest that there is nothing to fear at the time of death. It's merely a transition. Our soul knows its way home…to the Heavens.

Your Unseen Support Team is eagerly waiting to assist you. All you have to do is invite them!

- Whitedove

Dear Whitedove,
My best friend has been praying and she told me that she's looking for a sign or an omen that an opportunity will open up for her. I'm confused as to what kind of sign would be needed to convince her to go in a new direction?
- Jobless in Portland

Dear Jobless,
In communicating with the Divine, prayer is the method to communicate your issues and to give thanks. Once we hand our problems over, then we must be open to receive a solution. Meditation is the best way to listen for answers to your prayers. Asking for a sign or **omen** is the next best thing. These signs can be small, or they can be grand, but they always ring true when you understand that the message is for you. If your friend was insightful enough to ask for an omen then have faith that she'll follow the guidance.

Dear Whitedove,
I have taken photos of my young daughter and

there's an orb in several of them. From everything that I have read, this means that there is a spirit or a ghost of a loved one with her. How can I distinguish?
- *Photo Mom*

Dear Mom,
Indeed orbs are photographed frequently. Most orbs can be attributed to dust particles or moisture droplets: usually you will know because there's a multitude in the picture. Then there are orbs that are related to paranormal activity and soul travel. Usually there will be only one or two spirit **orbs** in these photos.

You see the soul is energy, so as light bounces off the sphere of energy the camera captures it on film. The most obvious indicator of a spirit orb is its swift movement in a direction that would be unnatural for dust or water. The Soul travels at the speed of thought so they move quickly from one realm to another. A spirit orb can represent a Guardian Angel, Spirit Guide, a fairy, a loved one or an Earth bound spirit.

Dear Whitedove,
I am interested in Spirit Communication and I'd

like to know how you feel about the Ouija board. I believe that it's just another tool but a friend of mine told me that these boards are evil. Do you think that it's OK to play the Ouija board?
- Need to know in Minnesota

Dear Needing,
As a teacher, I recommend to my students to "Go Directly to the Top." All spirit communication should be done through prayer and meditation by connecting with Father/Mother/God. When contacting the other side, you want to merge with the love and light of God where the information is pure and honest. I would also suggest communicating with your spirit guides and Guardian Angels for insights and guidance. If you wanted to connect with a specific departed loved one, I would recommend that you seek out a reputable "Spiritual Medium."

The **Ouija Board** is an unreliable tool that helps to open communication with ANY spirit, not necessarily ones of love and light. The board is not a toy so please do not play with it. Contacting the "Other Side" isn't a game, it's a privilege.

In the Heavens, fear and darkness
cannot exist.
Hell is right here on Earth!
- Whitedove

P

Dear Whitedove,
I heard this lady on the radio who said she was a pet communicator. Is it possible that there's a modern day Doctor Doolittle?
- Pet issues in Parker

Dear Pet issues,
Yes, some psychics do communicate with animals. This is done through telepathic connections. Some animals such as horses, dogs, and cats have very human-like thoughts making it possible for a pet psychic to interpret. Using a pet psychic is often the best way to resolve pet issues. I had a dog named Ashley who was very old and cranky and I was worried that she was in pain, but couldn't find the source of her discomfort. A pet psychic came to my house and told me that Ashley was upset that we had replaced our carpet with tile because it was cold and hurt her legs. I had in fact replaced all the carpets with tile six months prior. Armed with this information I was able to lay down some thick rugs to give Ashley the relief that she needed. If you plan to visit a **pet communicator** make sure you do your research and choose someone that's authentic. Since animals can't confirm these insights you will need to pay very

close attention and look for signs that would give you validation that the information rings true.

Dear Whitedove,
I have recently started dating a yoga instructor and whenever we have a meal together she insists on prayer. I am new to spirituality but I always thought that praying before a meal was a religious ceremony. I don't understand and I'm too embarrassed to ask her to elaborate. Please explain this to me?
- *Praying in Pensacola*

Dear Praying,
Our direct line to Great Spirit is through prayerful communication regardless of religion. **Praying over the food** that we eat is a way to give thanks to Great Spirit and the Earth for providing it. Prayer also creates change...even when it comes to food. Let me give you an example; I was eating dinner with a group of friends one night; I said a prayer over food as always, but no one else did. Five hours later every person that ate the meal became ill with food poisoning, except for me. Because of my faith in the power of prayer I was spared the discomfort of food poisoning. Prayer is a powerful tool and if you utilize it in your everyday

life you will be amazed at how much protection you will receive in all aspects of your life. You can pray out loud or silently; Spirit will always hear you. Learning to use prayer is the most important step to becoming spiritually aware.

Dear Whitedove,
Please enlighten us, my friend and I disagree as to why predictions from psychics are sometimes accurate and other times so off the mark. How can I explain it to him? Why would the information that's coming from "The Other Side" end up wrong?
- ***Seeker from Miami***

Dear Seeker,
There is only one being that is omnipotent, and that is the Great Spirit. There are several factors that determine the accuracy of a psychic message or **predictions**. First there is Free Will. Psychics "see" the most probable future. Many psychic messages that are relayed to clients are given as a warning, not a predestined fate. If a psychic tells someone that they have a car accident in their energy that's not to say it will happen for sure, it is supposed to help them be aware of the danger and do things to prevent an accident from occurring at all: buckle up, be more cautious, and

drive with awareness.

On global predictions: Due to the Free Will of all the billions of souls who are focused on the same global issues and unifying their thoughts. Future predictions can often be swayed according to what our collective consciousness is creating. The 2008 US Election is a perfect example of the collective consciousness in action. Remember, Psychics and Visionaries give predictions based on the most probable outcome at the time, BUT the future is always shifting!

Another thing to consider is that psychics glean their messages through communication with Great Spirit, their Angels and their guides. Great Spirit is never wrong but the reader can be. Heavenly Spirits do not have a set of vocal cords, so a psychic medium that is "plugged into" the divine intelligence receives the information as a "Knowing." If the readers' intellect or ego gets in the way, this will influence the information.

I'd like to remind you that everyone has intuition and psychic abilities, you have the answers within. Through prayer you are speaking to the Great Spirit, and once you practice the art of meditation, then you will begin to hear the solutions to your personal issues. God speaks to all of us, it's just that some people have forgotten how to listen.

Dear Whitedove,
How do you feel about prophetic dreams? Sometimes I dream of events still to come. Other times they are about people that I know, but are more symbolic rather than factual. It's all very confusing information. How am I supposed to interpret these wild dreams?
- *The Dreamer, Montreal*

Dear Dreamer,
The dreamtime is the doorway to the spirit world. As the body rests and rejuvenates, the soul is released. We do many things during the dreamtime. Sometimes we work out solutions to Earthly problems and our fears. This is also the time when we meet up with departed loved ones and continue our relationships. Dreams are also a way of self communication on a soul level.

You see, in the spirit world there is no linear time as on Earth; the past, present, and future are all one. Then there are probable futures too. Upon waking we can remember witnessing events, but in Earth time these events have not played out as of yet. Premonitions or **Prophetic dreams** are valid, but you have to learn to interpret them for yourself.

I suggest to all my students to keep a dream journal. Train yourself to remember your dreams, they're important. At bedtime start a little ritual. Place a glass carafe full of spring water on your nightstand near your head, this is not for drinking. You're using this water as a superconductor to help bring clarity to your dreams. When you lay down, ask your subconscious mind to move over. It helps to make the request because your mind acts as a filter. Say to yourself, "I want to remember my dreams, and I will remember my dreams." This positive reinforcement will impress your true desires upon your subconscious mind. Upon waking, don't jump right up; think about where you were. Ask yourself; what was just happening? Then jot down all the details of your dreams before getting out of bed. The more that you practice, the clearer your dreams will become. You will enjoy rereading your dream journal and come to a better understanding of your soul's dreamtime escapes.

Many inventors receive information in the dream state. Thomas Edison would take cat naps in his office while holding marbles. He would focus on a solution to an invention as he would drift off to sleep. When he reached a level of deep sleep his hands would relax, the marbles would drop on the wood floor and wake him. By using this method to startle himself awake he would be able to remember more information from the dream state. Mr. Edison holds the world record for 1900 patented inventions. He was able to perfect a method to help him remember his dreams.

Throughout biblical scriptures there are many instances of God and the Angels relaying special knowledge about events to come through dreams. This is an easy method for spirit communication. When God wants to give us an urgent warning or encourage us to take action, a prophetic dream is an inspiring tool.

Dear Whitedove.
I believe that I have a "Psychic Kid." How do you decipher a child's imagination, verses authentic spiritual abilities? My son is just 6 years old, and he says that he sees spirits, even animal spirits, including his beloved cat that is deceased. He isn't scared, in fact he's quite matter-of-fact, but I'm still concerned.
- Blue Ray Mum in Canada

Dear Mum,
There is a special group of souls that are being born right now. Have you noticed the high rate of infertility? God has ordained that only evolved souls are to born into this realm. They are the new leaders and teachers, the next evolution in human kind. These **Psychic kids** are "The Ones" who will bring forth solutions to save this planet. Your son is your teacher. He is more than a psychic; he's a natural medium that was born with the gift of spiritual communication. He can see Heavenly beings, departed loved ones, and also Animal spirits. Your son is actually seeing all these apparitions.

Please know that pets will often stay with us after they drop their physical form. Other animal spirits will also manifest for him. Native Americans call them Animal totems; each animal energy carries a message and a medicine.

As a caretaker of a special soul, it is your job to nurture his ability and to protect him. Give him spiritual books to feed his soul. Keep him away from negativity, and don't expose him to violent movies and video games. Keep him occupied with activities to encourage spiritual growth, music, dance, and art lessons. Involve him in community activities and giving. Yours is a job of grooming a humanitarian. Do your job well!

Dear Whitedove,
I'm confused by all new age terminology: psychic, medium, intuitive, and channel. I want to experience a "reading" but I'm not sure what type of person that will help me.
~Inquisitive in Montana

Dear Inquisitive,
First I'd tell you to get a personal recommendation from someone who has had a session before selecting a reader. I make the analogy: readers are like doctors, each one is at a different skill level. Some are still in training, others are specialists, and then there are quacks that don't really care, it's just a job for them. You should sit down with someone who has a good reputation, so you can come away with clarity.

The definitions are pretty simple, a psychic is someone who can read your energy, and can look into your past, present, and future. A **psychic-medium** can read your energy plus connect to souls on the other side. A channel is connecting to the divine, the Universal Consciousness, the Angel Kingdom, Spirit Guides and the Masters for higher spiritual knowledge. Everyone is intuitive so this term is used loosely and varies from person to person. Be sure to ask the reader about their gifts, so that you are assured that they have the skills that you are looking for in a reading.

Dear Whitedove,
I've been having these very unusual experiences and there doesn't seem to be any logical explanation. Among other things I will smell roses where there are none; I hear noises in my home when no one is around, or no one else seems to hear it. I need to know what is going on with me.
- Crazy in Little Rock

Dear Crazy,
What you're experiencing is **psychic sensing** called Clair audio / Clair visual. You are tuning into energies psychically and the information is coming to you in a variety of ways. When I experience my intuitive gifts it's a knowing from Spirit, but I also see, smell, hear and taste which helps me obtain the information with more detail. As your intuitive gifts increase so does your awareness of energies around you that others can't always sense. Mother Mary will often

make her presence known through the scent of fresh roses, even when there are no flowers. People who have Native American guides will often smell a hint of tobacco or sage. These scents come to them psychically as a confirmation that the spirit is around. Try to pay attention to these signs and journal them, not just what you are seeing or hearing psychically but also what you were doing at the time. While sometimes these occurrences are simply meant to be a confirmation or reassurance that our angels and guides are with us, they can also be warnings of impending danger so remember to honor your gift and use it in a positive way to help yourself as well as others.

I'd like to encourage everyone to
Shield-Up with prayer daily.
Humanity is out of balance, the
Earth is shifting and people are
acting out of character. So pray and
keep yourself in a state of Grace.
Pray for the World.
Pray for the innocent.
- Whitedove

Q

Dear Whitedove,
A friend told me that I should wear a necklace made of rose quartz because it would help me. Do you believe that stones can have a real effect on the physical body?
- Thinking Pink, Georgia

Dear Pink,
Today modern science knows that quartz crystals generate an electrical charge and vibrate when mechanical pressure is applied to them. **Quartz** is used in radios, computers, and watches. Gemstones have been used throughout history for their beauty and their power. The Talmud and the Bible both speak of specific gemstones used for protection that cover the breast plate of the high priest. Kings and Queens used them in their crowns and stones were set in their swords and aligned specifically to enhance fighting abilities and to protect the user.

Your friend has suggested pink quartz because it emanates qualities of unconditional love for the world, and self love. We can all use more love right now. Wear the pink quartz on a necklace with a long chain. For maximum benefit wear it over the heart chakra, and know that stones are most effective when resting against the skin.

Life lessons are not meant to be stumbling blocks. These events are spiritual building blocks for your soul's growth. Embrace your lessons, they will make you stronger.

- Whitedove

R

Dear Whitedove,
I am curious if you believe in palm reading or tea leaf readings. My friend and I went and had them done at a convention and the readings were accurate, but how is that possible?
- *Bewildered in Georgia*

Dear Bewildered,
Yes there are many divination tools; however I personally do not use anything other than Prayer and Meditation when I do readings. If done correctly and with integrity tools such as the lines on ones hand or a deck of cards can be very helpful. True Psychics gain their knowledge from the Great Spirit; however many do use tools of interpretation to assist them. Psychics can use an array of different divination objects to help them understand the information coming through; tarot decks, runes, water, mirrors, coffee grounds, and tea leafs just to name a few. I know a woman who reads "bones" the ancient way. She has a person pick out several small animal bones and toss them down, she then reads the messages the bones have given her; of course it isn't the bones that are actually leaving messages, it is Spirit. Really anything can be read because what the Psychic is truly doing is picking

up the energy around the person. These tools are used as windows to help them decipher what spirit is trying to say. I know many very gifted psychics that utilize divination tools not because it is necessary, but it is their preference. Others like me, we just use our telepathic and clairvoyant connection and give the information as we see and hear it from The Source. If the information that you received was accurate then the palm reader that you went to was legitimate, just know that individual psychics usually have unique work styles to conduct their **readings**.

Dear Whitedove,
As a nurse, I've recently been drawn to work with Reiki. If I promote this will it hurt my practice or enhance it?
- *RN in Roanoke*

Dear RN,
People that are drawn into the medical field are natural healers. With love and empathy you are in service to humanity. **Reiki** is one form of healing, I would suggest that you master it and move on to incorporate other modalities of healing also. I see that the study of herbs and acupressure will benefit your practice too. Incorporating

Eastern healing practices will enhance your work by leaps and bounds, Go for it!

Dear Whitedove,
All religions believe that they are the ONLY way to gain entry into heaven, and everyone else is wrong. Do you think that God has a favorite religion? If so, I'd like to know which one.
- *Questioning in the Midwest*

Dear Questioning,
There is one truth that runs through the fabric of all **religions**, which is the Universal Law of Love. If everyone would "love their neighbor" as they love themselves, the world would be a perfect place. There would be no war, prejudice, segregation, or starvation.

When I had my NDE (Near Death Experience) I became aware that there is no religion in Heaven, all was one. Heaven is a collective consciousness of great love. It resonates as overwhelming waves of immense love and angelic songs of praise.

So I would suggest that here on Earth that you come from

compassion and unconditional love. In this way, you will make a positive impact on every soul that you connect with no matter what religious practice you follow. When the world joins together in unconditional love towards their fellow man, the animal kingdom, and Mother Earth... then we will have paradise once again here on our planet.

Dear Whitedove,
I'm getting pretty disillusioned with my church and their archaic rules and hypercritical abuses. Why does God allow so many religions all claiming that their doctrine is the only way to Heaven? Wouldn't you say there's a better way?
- Churchgoer in NYC

Dear Churchgoer,
Interpretations of spiritual doctrines have been the cause of much war and bloodshed throughout the ages. **Religion** is a manmade system of rules and regulations that has created segregation, prejudice and limitations. However Spirituality is growth. As we evolve and grow we can expand our beliefs. The basic truths and principals are found in the Universal Laws and they apply to everyone. If everyone would live their life ethically, by The Golden

Rule (which is mentioned in many religious text) Then the world would be a perfect place, the paradise as God originally created. Remember: "Do unto others as you would have them do unto you."

Dear Whitedove,
My ex-military friend professes to be a remote viewer. He wants to teach me to find some type of target. I'm a bit intuitive, but all this talk makes me a little uneasy. Can people really have this power?
- *Observer in Oklahoma*

Dear Observer,
There are trained **remote viewers** and two types: Shamanistic and Military. This is a learned skill that Shamans have used since the beginning of time. In the 1950's the Russian military developed a technique to train psychic spies for espionage. Then the US government got involved too. These military men sit in a room, and psychically look for a military target. It's a much more economical way for the Government to spy and it can give clearer insights into the subject. You are gifted, but I'd like to suggest that you learn the spiritual method to remote view. This is when you send out a piece of your soul to

view a person, place or a thing with a pure intent. With practice you can master this useful psychic skill.

During the course of your lifetime,
you will touch thousands of people.
Some of you will touch millions.
So let your light shine bright
as you impact each soul.
Strive to make a difference.
- Whitedove

S

Dear Whitedove
I've decided to make my spare bedroom into a meditation room and I'm very excited. I have done most of the work; the only thing that I'm lacking is the altar. I've been told it is very important to have an altar but I'm so nervous, any advice?
- ***Needs Help in New Jersey***

Dear Needs Help,
Altars are a **sacred space** that you are dedicating strictly to The Great Spirit and your unseen support team. I have seen many different styles of altars and whatever you choose is fine as long as your altar is putting the Great Spirit first. Do not use an altar as a way to pray to lesser deities, your prayers will be heard and answered much quicker if you take them directly to the source, the God Head. It is good to always have white candles on your altar to light for those who are in need of prayers. Fresh flowers are a wonderful sign of your love and respect to God and your unseen support team. On a personal note Sage, Bear Root, and a small bottle of holy water are absolute musts for my altar because as a spiritual medium I have a lot of paranormal activity in my home so I clear and bless my house on a regular basis. Whatever things you decide to

add to your own altar will be fine, whether it be statues of angels, or stones and crystals, just as long as you make sure your altar represents your personal connection to the Great Spirit.

Dear Whitedove,
My husband and I have argued over the last two Christmas's what to tell our five year old twin daughters about Santa Claus. It is unpleasant and I would like to have a resolution for when next Christmas rolls around. I want to let them keep believing but my husband feels like it's a lie. Is there any way that we can be honest while still keeping Santa alive in their minds?
- *Truth hurts in Tulsa*

Dear Truth,
First of all, Saint Nicholas was a real person. He gave his entire fortune to the poor and needy and spent his life helping to feed and cloth the less fortunate. As we all know just because someone's physical body dies, does not mean that they are gone forever. We often call upon the saints, angels and other masters from the heavens to help us. Well as a parent you can tell your children that Santa

Claus is simply the "Spirit" of St. Nick that lives in many of us. St. Nick's spirit helps create Christmas miracles, and generosity that do give children toys and gifts when least expected. When you see a man dressed up as **Santa Claus** in the mall he is playing homage to the real St. Nick who is all around us during this season. This way you are not lying but you are allowing your children to embrace the Santa Claus tradition in a healthy way.

Dear Whitedove,
A friend of mine is Native American and told me to use Bear Root instead of Sage when I smudge my home, what do you recommend. And where do I find Bear Root?
- ***Burning in Wyoming***

Dear Burning,
Bear root is a wonderful protective plant that I happen to burn on a daily basis in my home. Bear Root possesses a very strong connection to Spirit and will lighten and cleanse your homes energy and protect you very well. You can find it on the internet; make sure the source is selling the hard root and not a powder. I suggest burning a combination of White Sage, Cedar, and Bear Root; sometimes I even throw

in some Sweet Grass for good measure. **Smudge** with the sacred incense of roots and herbs to uplift the energy of a person or a place.

Dear Whitedove,
I want to know if animals have a soul like humans? I believe that they do; sometimes I look at my cat and I think she is more like a person than an animal. I'm a huge activist in animal rights and I always try to tell people that they have souls but I'm always shot down.
- Soulful in San Diego

Dear Soulful,
Congratulations on your work for Animals. They are a special group of God's children and deserve the same love, respect and care as humans. Yes, they have **souls** but animals have their own kind of evolution since they are a part of the Angel Kingdom. Unlike humans who have an individual soul, animals have what is known as a "Hive" soul. This means that they belong to a group consciousness that governs them as a whole. When an animal dies it returns to the collective consciousness. As for your cat, she's probably what I refer to as a "Familiar", these animals

are very unique as they are more cognitively aware than normal. They tend to be in between our world and the Spirit world. Familiars usually come into a human's life to act as a companion helper.

Dear Whitedove,
I've been trying to work on my own personal mediumship abilities and sometimes I think that I can see and feel Spirits near by, but I'd like to know is there a way that I can bring Spirits to me? How can I communicate with them? Thank you for your insight.
- *Wanting to see, Miami FL*

Dear Wanting,
First, please know that every soul born into this world comes in with two guardian Angels and Spirit guides. The number in your unseen support team is based on your life mission. They are there with you at your side. Prayer and meditation are the only tools that you need in order to call upon them. With practice you will start to see them, feel them, know them and with the dedication of time your **spirit communication** skills will improve.

However, if you are looking to attract wayward spirits or ghosts to yourself I'm afraid I cannot help you. Wayward spirits are lost and confused souls that need help crossing over into the Heavens. I don't advise anyone to do this for mere curiosity or for amusement. As a spiritual medium it is my job to help these souls resolve their issues that keep them Earth bound. In my Ghost Stalker books I give educational information not only on different types of hauntings but also about the ghosts' Earthy life. Remember, ghosts were once living humans with mothers, siblings, friends and children of their own, and they deserve to be treated with respect and understanding. Also it's important to know that not all wayward souls are benevolent, and they can be violent causing potential harm to those living around them. Please if you are interested in the phenomena of ghosts then read about them. The only spirits that you should call upon are your helpers, ones that reside in the heavens.

Dear Whitedove,

Do Spirit Guides communicate with us in our dreams? When I have a burning issue with someone I get a vivid dream and it usually reveals the truth about the situation.

- *Spirit Seeker in MI*

Dear Seeker,

Sleep is a time when the soul is set free. We have the opportunity to do much work on the other side as the body is resting. You are working on your issues and fears in the dream time and are given solutions to your problems. We all do this as help is given by Great Spirit, Guardian Angels and **Spirit Guides.** Many times you will wake up with brilliant ideas which are inspired by your unseen support team. This is also the time when your loved ones can come visit you from Heaven, these dreams are actual meetings. Pay attention to your dreams as you awaken, when they are fresh. Write them down before they disappear from your memory because they are an important source of guidance.

Dear Whitedove,

My heart goes out to all the people who are suffering around the globe. I don't have much to offer financially but I would love to do more. Any suggestions?

- *Shaken in Nassau*

Dear Shaken,

Earth is going through many changes on all levels;

unfortunately this is causing a rise in natural disasters, political unrest, and the break down of society. We need to come together as a spiritual community and start reaching out to those **suffering** in stricken areas. Prayer may seem simple but it is one of the best ways to help. When large groups of people pray for an area then all of that energy goes there to help ease the pain. For natural disasters; give assistance in the manner you feel most prompted: offer your time to volunteer at a donation center, collect supplies, give financial assistance, and give your prayers. With love and light these cities stricken with disasters will begin to rebuild but it will be a very slow process. Give whatever you can and remember that positive thoughts and your kind actions go much further than you realize.

Giving Audience Messages in New York City

Our children are on loan from Heaven. These souls are with us for a short period of time. My prayers go out to parents that have lost a child. I assure you, you will see your beloved again.

- Whitedove

T

Dear Whitedove,
I've been trying to get my teenager to become more spiritually aware. I've tried giving him my books about spirituality, even taking him to some events but nothing seems to be helping. How can I get him to grasp some basic spiritual concepts?
~Needing Solutions in Orlando

Dear Needing,
Just be it! Being a spiritual example is the best thing that you can do. Live by example, counsel your **teenager** and listen to him. Live your life like a prayer. It's best not to force spirituality on your teen. You don't want to come on too strong. Instead of making him attend spiritual workshops I'd suggest that you take him to a New Age store and let him browse around on his own. Then see what he's drawn to and notice where his interests lie. Does he like crystals, sacred incense, or a specific type of book? I'd also suggest taking him to have his aura photography done; it's something very different and usually the photo comes with a little mini reading which will peak a teens curiosity. Try to show him that spirituality is a lifestyle. Incorporate the Universal Laws into daily conversation when addressing situations. You can talk about karma, the law of attraction

and all of the others. It's up to parents to lead by example. Slowly but surely your teen will find his own spiritual path.

Dear Whitedove,
I hate holidays with my dysfunctional family! How can I get through another Thanksgiving without a family feud?
- *Lots of Turkeys in Iowa*

Dear Turkey,
It's easy to complain, but you have to take responsibility for your part in family disagreements. Biological family ties are important. We each come into this life with karmic ties to our family members. They have lessons to teach and we have experiences to learn from. Family members are your teachers, so try to find the lessons.

This Holiday season I encourage you to work on healing these relationships. Its easy to fall into a rut and take for granted the very blessings that are bestowed. Every day we should give thanks and be appreciative for all our blessings from the mundane to the exceptional. **Thanksgiving** is a time to be grateful for all the abundance that Mother Earth provides: crops harvests that nourish us, animals and water that sustains us. Lets take the consumerism out of the Holidays and get back the basics of what is truly important: the love that you give, and the love that you receive. Also, be thankful for the family that you have.

Dear Whitedove,
In difficult times it's hard to stay on the right path without getting all freaked out! The world seems so out of balance with war, economic challenges, crimes, and crazy weather too. Any advice for the light workers?
- *Bright Light in SC*

My Dear,
It's all too easy to become distracted with the negativity but freaking out with stress and worry won't help. These days that we are living in will be a time of great change and upheaval. Change makes us uncomfortable, but getting out of our comfort zone is just what we need to do. The negative aspects of our world need to be wiped away to make room for the rebirth of higher spirituality in 2016. In **times of turmoil**, focus your time and attention on helping those in need. Offer your prayers, give your love freely, be of service, and stay connected to the Divine Intelligence

for guidance. Material goods will come and go, but your actions, thoughts, and deeds stay with you for eternity.

Our children are on loan from Heaven. These souls are with us for a short period of time. My prayers go out to parents that have lost a child. I assure you, you will see your beloved again.

- Whitedove

U

Dear Whitedove,
There was a UFO sighting here in Texas yesterday, and it made the news. My sister saw the lights in the night sky that was a perfect triangle formation, as did many others. There were also sightings in NYC during the same week. Then the naysayers come out with silly explanations, balloons from a children's party. Please tell me: are we visited by beings from other Galaxies?
- *Little Green Man in TX*

Dear Green Man,
It's very egotistical of humans to look up into the night sky, see the millions of stars and then presume that we are the only beings that God created. Let me assure you there are many races of God's children. Even here on Earth, we have many other forms of intelligent life like the mammals of the sea, and the animal kingdom too. The Star Beings are our brothers and sisters; just know that we all were created by the same Mother, Father, God. Some of these celestial beings travel at the speed of thought, while other beings use light ships that we call **UFO's**. It's important to be open minded, as these beings are making themselves known because they want to assist humanity.

Dear Whitedove,
In my studies I have read that the New Age will change everything? What in the Universe is going on?
- New Ager in Naples

Dear New Ager,
Yes, you are correct, in December of 2012 the Earth moved into direct alignment with the center of the **Universe**. This has happened before, and it will happen again, it is the Earth's natural cycle. Now with that being said; Humans will be evolving too, our DNA is being upgraded. With this new age of Enlightenment comes the clearing away of many of the old ways that are corrupt. I wrote about these times in the year 2000, in my book She Talks with Angels. I foretold of the increase of natural disasters, the financial empires of the world crashing, that manmade systems that are no longer working with us will be wiped away: the education system, the healthcare system, and corrupt governments. Recently in the news, there are civil wars in many countries; people want new rules and governments that are based on integrity and what is truly in the best interest of the people. You see, we ARE raising our vibration... the world wants Unity! During these times of change you can expect great upheaval. It's time to get back to the basics, prepare to

take care of your loved ones with their vital needs: water, a well stocked pantry, maybe a grill and a generator too. During times of great change you need to simplify your life and get back to the basics. I say: Pray for the best but be prepared with important essentials because it usually gets worse before it gets better. Just know that the age of enlightenment is here, the door is open and change is occurring for the betterment of the Universe.

Dear Whitedove,
My brother was fired from his job for an offence that he did not commit. The injustices just continue and we have been unable to get him reinstated at work. Why are the Universal Laws not working for him?
- *Broken-hearted Sister in Jersey*

Dear Sister,
The **Universal Laws** are God's Laws that are always in motion. When our loved ones are suffering, it's difficult to comprehend that adversity can be part of God's plan. Before your brother incarnated he planned some of these major hardships as lessons for his soul's growth. The Universal Laws are at work and they include Karma from this life and previous incarnations. His words, thoughts, and deeds are

manifesting with his intent. Sister, we all will reap what we sow; whatever we do unto others, we do unto ourselves. God's Laws never fail.

The act of giving is really
a gift to yourself.
Now is the time to give more!
- Whitedove

V

Dear Whitedove,
Is it more spiritually correct to be a vegetarian? If animals are God's creatures also, I sometimes feel incredibly guilty eating meat. Should I?
- Animal Lover in Lodi

Dear Lover,
Being a **vegetarian** is simply a choice. I'm told by spirit that your body will tell you what is best for you. Eons ago the animal kingdom volunteered to give up their lives to give substance to humans. This is how humanity became carnivores. Then the Native American's gave thanks with gratitude and took the lives with great care and respect. Today there are many sources of protein other than animal. The foods are unfortunately so processed that the vibration is extremely low so it's best to bless everything that you consume. With that said, go organic for better health. Whatever your choice may be, God honors your free will.

Dear Whitedove,
Something horrific happened to my wife when she was a child. After we married, she confided in

me about this event, something that changed her forever. Since knowing this truth, I have this urge to seek revenge for the wrongdoing. Please help me to come to a spiritual understanding about why bad things happen to innocent people.
- *Loving Her in WY*

Dear Loving,
God tells us that we are never given more than we can handle. Unchecked human emotions can lead one to spiral out of control and **vengeance** can fester and become so vile, that it is no better than the original horrific deed. I'd suggest that you place your focus on being productive and help your loved one to heal her wounds mentally, emotionally, and spiritually. You see, mankind has the unique attribute of miraculous inner strength to rise up and overcome. When bad things happen, these circumstances can be the catalyst for greatness. Out of immense suffering, we can turn stumbling blocks into building blocks. Out of suffering and tragedy, people have pushed through and profoundly reshaped the course of their lives, and in turn become advocates, lawmakers, and fresh voices to seek positive change for the betterment of humanity. We don't always know God's grand plan, however it's important to understand that every negative situation can produce something that's very positive.

Dear Whitedove,
I take great pride in my career, my home, and my body. I'm a good person who's into self improvement. Recently I began studying metaphysics, but I just don't understand why some spiritual philosophies teach that "life is an illusion"?
- *Seeking Knowledge in Idaho*

Dear Seeking,
Science has proven that every object in this world is a group of **vibrating molecules** much like a holographic image. So understand that even your physical body is not a solid mass. During the transition that we call death, you will drop this body. Metaphysics teaches that you are not your body; you are a consciousness made of wisdom and unconditional love. Only your soul consciousness will survive. Your current life, this physical existence is only a blink of an eye in all of eternity. So in this way, life is an illusion. The Earth-plane is a place where the soul incarnates for learning expeditions. Your true home is Heaven.

ASK Whitedove

Dear Whitedove,
This year I need to set my priorities and focus on what I really want out of life. I seem to get caught up in other people's drama. Can you give me a daily exercise to help me focus on what I want to create?
- *Good Girl in RI*

Dear Good Girl,
It's a new year which is the perfect time to create a new vision. As a co-creator of your reality it's important to actively participate in manifesting a positive future. With a pure intent, know what you want, then you can begin to visualize it, believe it, invoke it by talking about it, and then do the work needed to make your goals a reality.

To help focus, I'd suggest that you create a **Vision Board.** It's a collage of positive images and affirmations to help manifest your personal dreams. Vision boards are easy to make. First, get a piece of cardboard from an old box; cut it into a rectangle. Now you need images to glue onto it, be clear on what you want to manifest in the year ahead. What does your new life look like?

Use old magazines to clip photos and go to internet for specific pictures and print positive affirmations too. Divide your rectangle into four sections and paste a big photo of you right in the center. Utilize one quarter of the space for Love: tailor the photos and affirmations for your new vision. Use the second quarter for finances, career, and education. One quarter for Home and family. Use the last quarter for your vision of the world: what you can do to create a better world... even if it's only prayers and affirmations. Once you are finished with your collage, place it in a location where you will see it every day. Each day, drink in the vision of your future, repeat your affirmations. Then in your daily prayers, give thanks. Vision Boards are one method of concentrated focus that will help you to consciously create your future. I wish you much success!

Guardian Angels do not shape
our destiny; we alone are
responsible for that.
But Angels can create
opportunities in our life.
So ASK them to assist!
- Whitedove

W

Dear Whitedove,
I recently heard of a concept called "Walk in", basically where a soul steps out of their physical body allowing another soul to come in. Do you think there is legitimacy to this phenomenon?
~Just Probing in OR

Dear Probing,
Yes there is absolute validity to this phenomenon called a "**walk-in**." In a literal sense this is soul swapping. The physical body remains the same but inside there is a soul exchange. A new soul begins to reside within. "Walk-ins" usually occur in one of two ways: When a person undergoes a severe trauma, or during a coma. The soul of the person is unable or unwilling to continue on with that life so they agree to leave prematurely without physically dying and thus allowing another soul to come in and complete the mission, soul contracts, and karma. This is with approval from the Divine Intelligence, but it is a rare occurrence.

The eyes don't lie; they are the windows to the soul. "Walk-ins" are noticed by close friends and family members due to the persons the drastic change in personality, interests, likes, dislikes. Most times the new soul will even have talents that the original soul did not, but the "walk-in" phenomenon is extremely rare.

Dear Whitedove,
I keep losing my keys. I know that sounds ridiculous but I swear for the last two days I'll set my keys down and they will disappear and then show up in some random place hours later. What is going on?
- *Lost in Atlanta*

Dear Lost,
I've actually had very similar experiences happen to me. When things like losing your keys repeatedly or doors being unexplainably locked when you know you didn't lock them, it is time to take a better look at "Why" these things are happening. Usually it's a **warning** from your unseen support team that there is a danger. Whether they are warning you of a potential break in, or of an impending car accident; unexplained phenomena like these are trying to warn you of some sort of danger that is in your energy. Read the signs around you; as they are a big part of learning to work with your intuition. If you continue to lose your keys then try not to drive

around more then necessary. When you do have to drive envision white light around you and your car; pray and ask Spirit to watch over you. When that car accident leaves your energy you will no longer have disappearing keys I assure you! If you honor these signs you will save your self much grief and potential heart ache in the future.

Dear Whitedove,
For the year I've been having dreams about water: all different types of water from soothing lakes to violent tidal waves. What does this mean?
- *Splashing in Sarasota*

Dear Splashing,
Our dreams are messages and they have the ability to give us multiple types of information as signs, insights, premonitions, and even warnings. We work out many of our life issues while in the dream state. Dreams help us prepare for things to come as well as give us added insight into our own consciousness.

Water in particular relates to our emotional state. If you dream of a calm serene lake then this is the reflection of what you're feeling emotionally or what you would like to be feeling. If you dream of a tidal wave coming over the top of you then it probably means that you are feeling overwhelmed by life, or if it can also be precognitive warning that something emotionally overwhelming is heading your way in the near future. Pay attention to your dreams, keep a journal and compare your notes to the events in your every day life; you'll be amazed by all the parallels. Journaling will help you to learn how to better interpret dreams for yourself.

Dear Whitedove,
When my parents built their home in the 1960's it was recommended that they hire a "Water Witch" to mark the location to drill a well. My Mother is super religious so I was surprised when she told me this story. She is a believer because the man found a deep well aquifer. I'm curious to know how people can find water sources that are invisible.
- *Curious in MS*

Dear Curious,
Water dowsing is an ancient art dating back to biblical times. It's a gift that is passed down generation to

generation and it can also be learned. A dowser or **Water Witch** is someone who is sensitive to the subtle energy currents of water. Usually the person will use a metal rod or a stick as a direction finder. Held loosely, parallel to the ground, the rod will move and point towards water as they walk around a location. The dowser feels the sensation of the energy field. The current weakens as they walk away from the hidden water source and it's strongest along the route that the water flows underground. Dowsing also works with locating mineral deposits, petroleum, and even lost objects. The more the dowser practices, the more heightened their abilities.

Dear Whitedove
Like many before me I am asking the Big Question: Why am I here? Life is so hard and I feel all alone in this world. Why does God want us to suffer?
- *Lost in Las Vegas*

Dear Lost,
We come here to Earth by our own Free Will. The Creator does not force us to do anything. **Why do we come here?** You see this journey was custom tailored to your soul's needs. Each soul comes for many of the same

reasons: to learn how to love and how to receive love, to learn spiritual lessons, and grow spiritually. If we wanted it easy we would have stayed in the Heavens. Instead souls chose to come to physically experience emotions and lessons. If you did not experience hardships, how would you know Joy? If you did not experience fear, how would you recognize love and acceptance? If you did not experience betrayal, how would you understand loyalty? Just know that the key to all things is unconditional love. It will make life more joyful and fulfilled.

Dear Whitedove,
A US President once said that God chose him, based on that statement I have two questions. What part does God have in World Leadership?
- *Blogger, PA*

Dear Blogger,
Before a human soul incarnates we make a contract with GOD, it's an agreement of the tasks, lessons, and goals that we are working to complete. **World Leaders** are a rare group of souls who come to make a difference. As we know, some get off their path and make unscrupulous decisions. God has given humanity the gift of free will.

At any time we can change our "Ideal" and have leaders that uplift humanity.

Here in America our two-party system no longer works as the founding fathers created. Big business and monopolies are now running our country. Our government is corrupt and no longer works for the middle class and the poor. God will not interfere with our free will. It's up to us to step up to the plate and make the changes.

As a visionary and futurist, I give predictions based on the Most Probable Future. Even quantum physics tells us that there is always more than one possible future. Usually I see three possible outcomes to any situation. For the last two elections I predicted G.W. Bush as the winner, and those turned out to be very controversial wins. Even with my foresight I still went out and voted my conscious for another candidate, because I know that the future can change with enough souls joining together.

With that said, I don't claim to be an all knowing Oracle. It's not possible to be 100% accurate when looking into the future because human's have the gift of free will. The future is always shifting. Only God knows the true outcome and I'm just a humble messenger.

Dear Whitedove,
As I look around my small hometown and even through out the rest of the world I see things becoming worse and I worry. I've been looking for ways to help humanity but I have little money and I'm a stay at home mom with very little free time. What can I do to help to make a difference?
- *Helpful in Xenia*

Dear Helpful,
Yes the world is in crisis and we are in a time of great change but there is always hope because we still create our own reality, but it has to start with each individual person. **Worrying** is like praying for the negative to happen. My suggestion is to give money to the poor and important causes, if you have no money then volunteer your time to charity, but if you have no time or money... then offer your prayers. Prayer is the single most powerful tool that we have. It's not just about asking Spirit for something, it's about concentrating our thoughts and words to help raise the vibration for yourself and those around you. Then visualize the world as you want it to

be, and hold that vision. To you and anyone else that would ask me this question, I would say Prayer is free, so if you truly wish to make a difference then just Pray! Dwell in the positive because you are a co-creator of this reality.

Dear Whitedove,
As an LPN my job is to help others heal. Many times it's not only a physical healing, patients will sometimes reveal very personal emotional issues too. Now there's a psychological and spiritual healing that's needed too. I feel that I'm very good at my job, but someone commented that I am a wounded healer. Would that explain why I'm not so keen on attending to my own health needs?
- Healer in WI

Dear Healer,
Most people that are humanitarians relate to people as an empathic, but in your case, you connect to your patients on even a deeper level. You my dear are a **Wounded Healer**. This means that in your "Soul Contract" you chose to experience some very difficult lessons. Not so much for your own growth but so that you would

shave first-hand knowledge to help others. A wounded healer can relate because of their own experiences. Many times these hard knocks are the very catalyst to help others. Your empathy, guides you to understand the patients issues on an intuitive level. Many Healers and Psychic Mediums have this common thread: they have overcome many major obstacles such as illness, abuse, abandonment and even atrocities. As they work through their issues they become victorious instead of a victim. These lessons were planned so that you could become your patients' teacher. As a healer, once you understand your soul's need to experience these hardships then you will want to care for and even pamper yourself. Make yourself a priority, you deserve it! You have to take care of yourself first in order to take care of others and continue work as a healer.

Story time in Weston, Florida

Your Random Acts of Kindness
go a long way. Even small gestures
make a big difference.

- Whitedove

X Y Z

Dear Whitedove,
Usually I plan my day according to my daily zodiac forecast. Now I'm starting to feel a little confined by my cautiousness. How closely should I follow my chart?
- *Gemini Girl*

Dear Gemini,
The **Zodiac** is made of Star constellations that you move through during the course of your life and you'll be uniquely affected according to your date, location and time of birth. There are many types of Astrology to use as predictors while on the Journey of the Soul: Chinese astrology, Vedic Astrology, Mayan Astrology, and Western Astrology all of these ancient systems were devised to enhance your life, not impede it.

Even if there's a negative aspect in your chart, you can lessen its impact by being proactive. This knowledge is not given so you can fret over it or focus on it so intently that you manifest the worst cast scenario. Remember, God has the first and last say. Your free will and through God's grace you have the ability to override your chart and create a better path. Very little of your destiny is written in stone. You are the Creator of your reality, so live your life to its fullest potential!

Photo Credit: Christine Kilger

Author's Biography

Celebrity Psychic & Spiritual Medium Michelle Whitedove was awarded the title of America's #1 Psychic, after proving her supernatural abilities on Lifetime Television. She has been tested on TV more than any other Medium. With humor and straight forward style Whitedove relays messages from the Heavens. As a sought after expert and gifted teacher, this six time author shares her Angelic messages of love, hope, and transformation.

Whitedove is top of her field and has been featured on TV around the globe: the TODAY Show with Matt Lauer, the HBO documentary No One Dies in Lily Dale, Lifetime TV's America's Psychic Challenge, MUN2, ABC, CBS, NBC, CNN, City TV, Sony TV, Breakfast TV and PBS TV. Currently she's on The Sixth Sense International on RTL TV Netherlands. Most recently she gave a reading to Patti Stanger, STAR of BRAVO TV's Millionaire Matchmaker and was invited to the TRISHA Show to walk through a haunted residence and give expert testimony as to who is haunting the home and why.

Michelle Whitedove teaches workshops, lectures across the globe. For more information go to

www.MichelleWhitedove.com

Follow her on TWITTER, Facebook, YouTube and Vimeo

Call upon your Guardian Angels
and invite them to help you.
They honor your free will
and they await your permission.
- Whitedove

Index

Index

Index

Index

Index

T

U

V

W

X, Y, Z

Gratitude brings many blessings.
Be thankful today and every day!
- Whitedove